Transportation
for the Poor

STUDIES IN APPLIED

REGIONAL SCIENCE

TRANSPORTATION FOR THE POOR

Research in Rural Mobility

HAL S. MAGGIED

Academic Director
Management and Administrative Studies
Career Development Center
Nova University

FOREWORD BY
WILLIAM E. BIVENS, III

AFTERWORD BY
JOHN S. HASSELL, JR.

KLUWER • NIJHOFF PUBLISHING
BOSTON/THE HAGUE/LONDON

DISTRIBUTORS FOR NORTH AMERICA:
Kluwer Boston, Inc.
190 Old Derby Street
Hingham, Massachusetts 02043, U.S.A.

DISTRIBUTORS OUTSIDE NORTH AMERICA:
Kluwer Academic Publishers Group
Distribution Centre
P.O. Box 322
3300 AH Dordrecht, The Netherlands

Library of Congress Cataloging in Publication Data

Maggied, Hal S.
  Transportation for the poor.

  (Studies in applied regional science)
  Bibliography: p.
  Includes index.
  1. Rural poor — United States — Transportation.
I. Title. II. Series.
HE203.M28   362.5′83   81-15571
ISBN 0-89838-081-2   AACR2

CONTENTS

LIST OF FIGURES

LIST OF TABLES

FOREWORD

William E. Bivens, III

For the first time in more than 160 years, the nation's rural areas and small towns are growing faster than its metropolitan areas. The 1980 Census of Population shows that the nonmetropolitan population increased by 15.4% during the 1970s, while the metropolitan population grew by only 9.1%. During the 1960s, rural areas and small towns had lost some 2.8 million people to cities and their suburbs, but during the 1970s at least 4 million more people moved into nonmetropolitan areas than left them. This rural-oriented population growth resulted from a number of factors, including a strong preference for rural and small-town living, the decentralization of manufacturing and related services, energy and other mining developments,

William E. Bivens, III, is the Senior Policy Fellow for Rural Affairs of the National Governors' Association. He is a rural development generalist providing liaison between the governors and federal officials and performing applied policy research to support improvements in rural development programs and systems for their delivery.

Mr. Bivens was one of the designers of the Carter Administration's Small Community and Rural Development Policy and provided the implementation link involving the formation of governors' rural development councils.

Mr. Bivens attended Brown University and did postgraduate work at the University of Texas, where he also taught American government and politics.

and comparatively high rural birthrates along with improved infant mortality rates.

Although a significant amount of recent nonmetropolitan population growth is accounted for by the continuing urbanization of exurban fringe areas around metropolitan cities, many more remote mining and resort-retirement areas have also experienced hyperurbanization. Both types of growth, exurban and remote, have been a mixed blessing. The impacts on the natural environment, local institutions, public facilities and services, social pathology, and the cost of living often have been negative, and many long-time residents have failed to benefit from the growth that has occurred.

At the other extreme, despite the relatively widespread nature of recent rural growth, about 485 nonmetropolitan counties, mainly in the Great Plains, the western Corn Belt, and the Mississippi Delta, have experienced population decreases during the 1970s. In these counties farming tends to be a major source of income and employment, and a continuing loss of farm population has not been offset by nonfarm development.

On the one hand, countryside and village life is becoming more urbanized in both a demographic and a cultural sense. On the other hand, the problems of physical isolation and poverty persist for many rural Americans. Rural areas are still characterized by dispersed populations and small-scale communities. Their institutions and people still face the problems of adapting for their own use urban-oriented technologies premised on economies of large scale that tend to be achievable only in a more densely populated setting without benefit of offsetting revenues. Rural residents still are disproportionately poor, ill-housed, chronically ill or disabled, and otherwise disadvantaged. Too many rural Americans have been left behind by whatever progress has occurred, and too many rural communities lack the fiscal wherewithal to finance developmental projects. As Dr. Maggied posits, and so succinctly reports in his findings, a symbiosis as well as a correlation does exist between rurality and poverty. His comparative analyses quantitatively display the dynamics.

Despite the filtering down of industry to rural areas, over two million rural workers commute from a minimum of 25 to 30 miles one-way between their homes and metropolitan workplaces. Dr. Maggied's incisive research has discovered some commuter trips extending 90 miles. Fuel costs and availability are a special concern for these and millions more rural people who must rely on private vehicles to get to work substantial distances from their homes. The striking fact, as Dr. Maggied found, is that less than 1% of rural Americans who work away from home use public transportation to get to their jobs. Only those who reside in about 315 of the nation's 20,000 nonmetropolitan municipalities are served by a public transit system. Only about half the country's small towns and minor cities have even intercity bus service.

The dependence of rural Americans on the private automobile or light truck is stark; yet 15% of rural households do not own a car, and 52% have only one, implying that some family members may well be left isolated and immobile for considerable periods. The problem is particularly severe for the rural poor, 57% of whom do not have a car, and for the rural elderly, 45% of whom do not own a car.

When one addresses the transportation problems of the poor, the rural poor must constitute a major focal point. About 62% of the nation's poor live in nonmetropolitan areas. The nonmetropolitan poverty rate is 13.7%, while that for metropolitan areas is 10.6%. The 9.6 million rural poor have substantially less access to public transportation than do their metropolitan peers; yet they have much greater distances to travel in order to commute to work, obtain essential services, and make necessary purchases.

The problems of rural isolation and the plight of the transportation disadvantaged in rural America have been recognized by some public officials for well over a decade now. For example, in November 1968 the Office of Economic Opportunity (now the Community Services Administration and slated for extinction by President Reagan) sponsored a conference on rural transportation focused on the needs of the poor, and in December 1969 the federal Bureau of Public Roads published *The Transportation Needs of the Rural Poor*. By 1973 enough concern had been generated at the federal level and enough experience had been gained with rural paratransit at the local level to prompt enactment of a program of grants in support of "rural highway public transportation demonstrations" and authorization of capital equipment grants and loans for nonprofit corporations providing rural transit services for the elderly and the handicapped. Previously, the federal government had supported rural transit or paratransit primarily indirectly, through social service programs that allowed provision of transportation services for their clients. Under such an arrangement, most rural transit providers were community action agencies and area agencies on aging, rather than local governments.

Seven years have passed now since Claude S. Brinegar, then the federal secretary of transportation, pointed out that rural public transportation policy was in an uncertain state, with numerous isolated rural areas accessible only by private conveyance. At that time, Bruce Lentz, then the secretary of transportation for North Carolina, charged that federally assisted transportation programs were largely unresponsive to rural development and that the federal transportation funding posture was biased against rural states. During the past seven years, the federal government has accorded more attention than previously to the mobility problems of rural Americans. However, we now face a fiscal retrenchment at the federal level that could result in a reversal of policy. Rural Americans are likely to be left to their own devices in the transit field once again.

Unfortunately, the policy linkage between rural passenger transportation needs and broader rural development concerns has been rather slow in coming. In fact, progress in this direction probably would have been much slower if it were not for the work of a few individuals at the Office of Economic Opportunity; the Department of Health, Education, and Welfare; and the Department of Transportation during the early 1970s. Perhaps more important in publicly exposing the issues, however, was the work of the Senate Subcommittee on Rural Development, then chaired by Senator Richard Clark of Iowa, and the House Subcommittee on Family Farms and Rural Development, then chaired by Congressman William Alexander of Arkansas. With support from Senator Herman Talmadge of Georgia, who simultaneously chaired the Senate Committee on Agriculture and Forestry, numerous hearings were held and many committee prints were issued on rural transportation problems during the early to mid-1970s. However, only with the OPEC oil embargo was there much focus on the problems of rural commuters.

Prior to the congressional efforts, the principal transportation concerns of most rural development policymakers related only to freight transport, particularly with regard to agricultural commodities. Most viewed the construction and improvement of rural roads and bridges as the answer to rural immobility. This policy perspective reflects the nature of supporting staff work at the time. For example, in the early 1970s, when the Economic Research Service of the U.S. Department of Agriculture reported on transportation and rural development, it focused on transportation as an industrial location factor and could muster no more than 385 words of generalization on the subject in response to congressional inquiry. Such was the recognized state of the art, generally. To be sure, Dr. Maggied's disclosure of unpaved roads as an inhibitor for commuters to work stations is a new approach to ascertaining the extent of rural poverty. This disclosure has brought the traditional concern for rural roads a new meaning related to the incidence of rural poverty. The poor are the least likely to get their rural roads paved.

Attention to the journey-to-work problems of rural Americans has been relatively sparse both in the literature and in the policy arena, although a few studies in the late 1960s and early 1970s dealt with the subject, and more has been done since then. Dr. Maggied's work is part of what would be a rather short bibliography, even with the additional attention accorded this issue since the OPEC embargo.

At the federal level, there generally has not been a specific institutional focal point for dealing with rural commuting needs within the context of overall rural development concerns. Creation of the Rural Development Service within the USDA provided a much needed, albeit temporary, organizational vehicle for dealing with such issues as the relationship between rural development and rural passenger transportation. However, this small agency lost identity when it was merged into the Farmers Home Administration, and it lost its transportation function to a new Office of Transportation within the department. The result over time has been a return to more or less singular emphasis on commodity transportation within the USDA, despite the department's broad rural development mission.

The U.S. Department of Transportation has done little more. Not only has it historically allocated only about 1% of its transit funding to rural America, its Office of Rural Transportation Policy has been a very small operation with only an advisory role. Although part of the Office of the Secretary, this five-year-old token has not had the influence necessary to serve the interest of rural America in the face of competing urban demands — particularly for the poor and, certainly, for the nonworker.

One result of the executive branch's reluctance to make a strong commitment to meeting rural transit needs was a twenty-five-month hiatus in specific federal program support. Several months after the expiration of the Section 147 demonstration program, the Carter Administration's position was that the results were inconclusive. Concerns about rural development needs had not surfaced yet in the White House Office of Intergovernmental Affairs and certainly had not captured strong support from the secretary of transportation, although he stated that rural areas should enjoy the same flexibility as cities do in using Urban Mass Transportation Administration funds for operating expenses. Overall, the reader need only review Dr. Maggied's chapter on legislative history regarding the poor and rural America to see quite clearly that these issues have been neglected individually and obscured collectively. It is only recently that federal transportation programs have begun to address the problem from a people-oriented, holistic approach.

For example, in November 1978 President Carter signed into law the Surface Transportation Assistance Act of 1978, which authorized a new federal program to support rural transit. This formula-grant program, "Public Transportation for Nonurbanized Areas," marked the beginning of a broader and firmer, albeit transitory, federal commitment to meeting rural transit needs. It was one of the least controversial portions of the legislation as it moved through the Congress, reflecting its focus on administrative simplicity and flexibility and the coordination of federally sponsored rural transportation, as well as recognition of the needs of the rural transportation disadvantaged.

Although the Section 18 program moved federal support for rural transit out of the research and demonstration phase, it did little to integrate rural transit with federal programs beyond those assisting transportation services. State transportation agencies were the USDOT's preferred vehicle for program administration, and emphasis in the regulations was on coordination with other transportation providers and social service agencies. Only five governors designated agencies other than those responsible for highways or broader transportation activities. Thus, coordination with other important state-level rural development activities, such as community development technical assistance, generally must be through interagency arrangements, which essentially are voluntary. Generally, though, as Dr. Maggied discovered in his analysis of "carlessness" and "phonelessness," the USDOT displayed insensitivity, if not hostility, toward rural situations.

In December 1979 President Carter announced his Small Community and Rural Development Policy. This landmark recognition of rural needs by the nation's chief executive articulated a commitment to work toward addressing the rural problems of distance and size. Dr. Maggied addresses these problems adroitly in his discussions of sparsity in the urban hinterlands. Overcoming the problems of isolation from job sites, social services, and the government; reducing the dependence of rural residents on the private automobile; and addressing the special problems of rural entrepreneurs in gaining access to raw materials and markets because of transportation problems were specifically identified as policy objectives on rural initiatives.

As part of the arrangements for implementing the president's rural policy, a federal Working Group on Small Community and Rural Development was established by resuscitating a dormant group set up during the Nixon Administration. The assistant secretary of transportation for policy and international affairs was appointed to represent transportation interests, and a subordinate interagency task force on rural transportation was set up with his deputy as the chairman. Most of the activity concerned continuation and monitoring of previously announced initiatives.

Shortly after President Carter announced his rural policy, the congressionally mandated Rural Transportation Advisory Task Force issued its final report. Given their mandate, the task force primarily focused on agricultural freight transport; thus the federal government had missed an opportunity to examine rural transit needs.

In September 1980 President Carter signed the Rural Development Policy Act of 1980, the first major rural development legislation enacted at the federal level since 1972. The act strengthens the responsibility of the federal secretary of agriculture for supporting rural development efforts, and it mandates preparation of a comprehensive rural development strategy for fiscal 1982. The Reagan Administration, however, has been granted a one-year extension to submit its strategy. If budget is considered to represent policy, the likelihood is that the strategy will contain little positive support for meeting rural transportation needs and none, essentially, for people transit.

Also, at the same time, the USDOT issued its "Proposed Policy Initiatives for Small Community and Rural Transportation," in response to President Carter's Small Community and Rural Development Policy. This rather limited document failed to address rural road and bridge problems, rail branch-line abandonment, or small-community air service needs in an adequate fashion. The emphasis was on technical rather than financial assistance, and regulatory reform was promoted as beneficial rather than detrimental to rural areas, despite the evident impacts of deregulation. Assuredly, issues regarding impact on mobility of the poor through "free" pricing mechanisms were not addressed.

Ronald Reagan won the 1980 presidential election and became the nation's fortieth president. The macroeconomic policies of the Reagan Administration have translated into proposals for massive budgetary reductions and program terminations that would severely afflict rural America's elderly, handicapped, and poor. The administration's philosophical position that the federal government should get out of certain program areas has made the state role in rural development and rural transit all the more important. This position reveals vast disparities among states regarding the role they choose to play.

Few state governments provided substantial aid for rural transit until the late 1970s, although most offered capital or operating assistance by the middle of the decade. Some state involvement in rural transit preceded enactment of the Section 147 program in 1973, but the state role was not substantial until the Section 18 program got under way. This is not to say that some states had not adopted strong roles before 1978 or that the state presence was not growing generally. In fact, the Section 147 program and provisions of the National Mass Transportation Assistance Act of 1974 stimulated greater state interest and involvement, as did the USDOT's communitywide transit development program requirement initiated in the spring of 1976 for rural services funded under Section 16(b) (2).

Dr. Maggied describes research in several states that is worthy of examination and reports that overall little state programmatic activity existed as late as 1976. He also points out the apparent lack of interest in the transit needs of rural work-trip commuters, a phenomenon at the state level that reflected the situation at the federal level.

Given political pressures to assist transit in major cities, most states have tended to become financially involved in rural transit only with the advent of federal programs. Prior to the Section 147 program, state involvement was almost solely through administration of federally funded human service programs. However, a few early state efforts laid much of the groundwork for subsequent rural transit activities, where they played a major role in assisting, coordinating, and otherwise fostering the implementation of the Section 147 demonstrations. The federal budgetary retrenchment, however, forces state officials to question the future of rural transportation for the poor.

To put it bluntly, there is little prospect for improved or increased transportation services for the poor, particularly in rural areas. In fact, in their efforts at fiscal retrenchment, policymakers may stumble upon the fact that disallowing transportation costs under various human service programs would cut costs quite substantially by not only eliminating transportation funds but also significantly reducing effective demand for basic services by the transportation disadvantaged. Without general-purpose transit aid, particularly operating subsidies, from the federal level, many paratransit and even small, conventional transit systems are likely to be highly dependent on contracts with human service agencies. Without such contracts, prospects for economic viability are quite limited. As Dr. Maggied notes, relying on private enterprise will render grave diseconomies to the operator and, ultimately, disservice to the rider.

The politics of retrenchment and the eventual electoral approval or disapproval of current budget cutting will determine not just where the poor go from here, but whether they must go on foot. For the nonfarm working poor in rural America, it can mean the difference between access to a living wage and continued poverty. For the elderly and disabled, virtually total isolation is a very real prospect—a sad prospect, indeed.

A nation that can build and fly a space shuttle should be able to provide transportation services for its poor, if not mitigate poverty.

PREFACE

When one engages in research, necessity usually requires the researcher to reduce the world to manageable size and then to shape it in order to promote understanding; one must shear away any feelings that might bias the research so it can withstand rigorous testing in achieving and maintaining replicable empiricism. Yet, given the human condition, researchers bring their experience with them in whatever they do, even as they observe a phenomenon and suspect a problem — the first step in the scientific method. While the procedures followed in this project certainly are according to the discipline mandated in any research design or methodology text, many events throughout my lifetime conditioned my thinking about mobility of the poor. Ultimately these concepts wove the fabric of this design.

These two aspects, experimental and professional, may be taken separately or together. Regarding the former, for instance, as a child who grew up in the thirties without benefit of bicycle or "motorized" mother, I constantly daydreamed of little motorized "dodge-em" types of car that would be available from bedroom to classroom. In retrospect, the dream was not entirely far-fetched. Today, although they are sparse and wheel-less, these individualized conveyances are referred to by the experts as people-movers.

The desire for individuals to own ancillary locomotion is obviously not a recent phenomenon. Prior to the automobile and the motorcycle, most people had or wanted a horse, a source of power and speed. The nomenclature used to identify vehicle power today is still measured in "horses." But not everyone could own a horse, nor today can all people own cars. Despite the fact that over 80% of American households own at least one car, nearly 20% of the households do not have access to any. It has been argued that many householders do not want a car because public transit serves them well. This argument may be valid to a degree in compact urban areas, but this research indicates otherwise; those who are carless by choice comprise a very small proportion of the carless household population. In fact, this research shows that householders who are carless are so essentially because they are poor. They are often so poor that they are without a telephone — in an era when instant communication is considered by most to be ubiquitous. This sense of ubiquity is fallacious and a source of many problems in understanding the "hard-core" nonemployed and the permanently impoverished.

Growing up during the Great Depression, I made many cursory observations about automobile ownership. Many of those observations were influenced by adult statements — conventional wisdom, such as: The poor always buy expensive used cars when they would be better off buying smaller, cheaper cars. As our family business was retailing "cheap" transportation from the automobile salvage yard, I perceived that the poor — our family's customers — operated under this irrationality. It appeared that the poor usually bought big, costly-to-operate vehicles.

Although this study will not analyze the behavioral side of economics, it is clear that the same people who were restricted in their residential location and priced out of adequate housing by "redline" rules often found the big automobile a basis of prestige and status.

Our family's primary source of cars to sell was the used-car dealer on the "avenue," who did not want big cars on his lot because they typically absorbed valuable space as slow movers. Salvage (junk) yards, on the other hand, generally were adjacent or proximate to low-income residential areas. Thus their kind of business fed inner-city customers, poor whites and poor blacks, with vehicles inappropriate to their income. Why didn't they select smaller, efficient cars? Because most of the good cars were sold on the avenue at higher prices. The others, usually less expensive, were battered, rusted, or just plain worn out and not suitable for dependable operation.

Many of the poor were not native to the industrial heartland's central cities; rather, they were part of the continuous migrant wave from rural to urban America that sought high-income jobs in factories. The poor of the country came to the city.

A large proportion of these ex-farm workers and nonworkers were carless. These migrants, in part, were so-called hillbillies and rednecks, who suffered humiliation and denigration as the subject of jokes about their culture, habits, appearance, housing, and transport. Generally, they were the offspring, siblings, and, in some cases, parents of scattered residents who were from areas caught in chronic depression, who so often were found wanting for mobility and access to jobs in order to share in a part of the American mainstream.

This striving for mobility is not unique to Americans. Those in the military occupation forces in Korea noted a similar phenomenon. Poor workers commuted inordinately long distances to seek and hold jobs, often under precarious conditions. In Cholla Nahm Do Province, I was assigned as an alternate dispatcher and driver. The first run every morning and the last run at night were to pick up and drop off, respectively, day workers from the "nearby" town. Most of these day workers were refugees from the North of a war-ravaged occupied country. They usually accepted any work assignment. They were hired by the military government to work in the civilian compound of the camp and were carried by the typical "deuce'n-a-half" cargo and personnel carrier. Since no intracity transit system existed and the intercity bus was quite costly as well as operationally infrequent, the military became the interurban carrier. Unlike the comfort that the troops enjoyed when seated at capacity of twenty, the fifty to sixty native riders had to endure extremely crowded conditions as standees for over nine miles, transiting on improved but unpaved byways through winding, hilly terrain in all kinds of weather. Needless to say, the trip for the passenger was less than optimal in terms of time, safety, and comfort.

A second revelation of that phenomenon was seen in Pampanga Province, Luzon, also a rural poverty area. The work-trip commuting demand was significant enough to encourage jitney service from the remote reaches to urbanized centers. The trips generally were lengthy in distance and time. Much of the travel was on substandard roads in converted jeeps and weapons carriers. To exacerbate the commuters' problems, the total trip could cost nearly 30% of their daily wages if the end-to-end trip required two transfers.

As one pursued the study of transportation organizations in the early 1960s, it was clear that most experts in this area of study were interested mainly, if not solely, in cargo movement. People movement was an overlooked but significant field of research. An early motivation for this research came from my program adviser. A question he posed often was, Is the federal government subsidizing the auto industry, exurban developers, and construction interests by linking its highway laws with interacting monetary and housing policies? By coupling this question with the notions of my economics major professor about impacts on the poor deriving from legislative enactments and regulatory policy by all levels of government, the problem was clarified substantially but not completely. Myriad poverty problems were erupting from urban renewal due to slum clearance displacement; patchwork relocations of the dispossessed on the periphery of the civic centers and along the freeway corridors allowed minimal relief from the boiling demographic cauldron. One thing was certain: the poverty issue surfacing in urban America in the early sixties was little more than a transplant of rural problems burgeoning during the first half of the twentieth century. Additionally, the harshness and meanness of ghetto life compressed these transplanted rural folk to a point of critical mass in close-quarter tenements that triggered the missile. It simply exploded. Those left behind were still left behind.

Concurrently, personal transit services were declining. But this decline was viewed by policymakers and public administrators only in the context of moving the affluent commuter initially from the suburb to the urb, and now to other gentrified suburbs. Speedy freeways allowed easy access to rural residency: exurbia and concomitant urban employment. The poor, however, particularly in rural America, were seldom given any consideration, if ever much thought, when policy recommendations were enunciated.

Several years later, this point began to gnaw at me. While exploring conditions in Appalachia concerning economic development and activity location, the research group interviewed managers who said that plant accessibility for workers was not a problem. Yet their regional labor force participation rates fell below the national and state averages; median educational attainment was under the national and state levels; and health conditions did not measure up to national and state standards. Couple these deficiencies with the single factor that many of the depressed areas targeted for improvement under the redevelopment acts had sunk deeper into the morass. Something was wrong, but what had they overlooked?

At the onset of the oil embargo in 1973, studies in which I was engaged brought home the message of the oversight. One, a transportation land-use model study, revealed that amid the settlement pattern of exurban sparsity, a scatteration of poor and near-poor remained. The other, a study of transportation investment on economic development, conveyed concerns of work-trip commuting costs to low-income householders, specifically long-distance commuters. At first, when they began to hear questions from Area Planning and Development Commission directors about transportation subsidies for commuters to work sites, the researchers dismissed them as an insidious, localized problem. As the oil embargo wore on and petroleum prices doubled, however, the question proved more perplexing. It seemed that what they had dismissed in their research as insignificant and inconsequential was, to the contrary, salient, prevalent, and pervasive.

Thus, when I was given the assignment to determine Georgia's statewide transportation needs under the Section 147 demonstration project, it was possible to reexamine previous research to find that planners typically assessed transportation costs only for physical resources and materials, not for humans; transport time was studied for style or spoilage, not for human comfort. Moreover, further investigation revealed that most of the work on commuter costs was done by social and health planners rather than by economic or manpower planners. The little work that had been performed either did not utilize the variables that were determining factors (and later used in this research) or it did not link the measures or variables as they had been in the model. To be sure, the data do not engender instant understanding nor do they enhance precise and rapid analysis. But escalating transport costs were upon the economy and society, and the polity needed some method for identifying the mobility disadvantaged.

Therefore, the document you are about to read brings together nearly two decades of experience and observation bedeviled by fallacy and obfuscation within the policy formulation system. It was evident that a theoretical base postulated human resources as being expendable parts of the socioeconomic infrastructure. There are those who hold that people are the highest form of capital and thus deserve a greater degree of emotional, intellectual, and financial investment than we have seen thus far. Such a perspective is intended to be revealed as an essential bias in this study.

ACKNOWLEDGMENTS

I express my thanks to Al Linhares and Norm Paulhus of the U.S. Department of Transportation, Office of Technology Sharing, Division of Systems Research.

The results of this research would not have been as encompassing nor pervasive without the counsel, guidance, perception, and patience of Professor Frank Gibson, Director, Graduate Studies for Public Administration at the University of Georgia. His stimulation helped me to persevere with a knotty problem that has been overlooked and obfuscated by service providers in the field of economic policy analysis and transportation planning. As a consequence of his ready availability to confer with me as new issues arose, the scope of this book expanded regarding examination of personal mobility for rural denizens.

Many thanks to due also to Dr. Del Dunn, Director, Institute of Government, Dr. Ernie Melvin, Director, Institute of Community and Area Development, and Professor Jim Wheeler, Chairman, Geography Department,

The University of Georgia. Also, many thanks to Professor Dave Billings, Director, Graduate Studies for Business Administration, Professor Everett Lee, Director of Behavioral Research, and Professor Charley Floyd, Chairman, Regional Economics Department. Their advice left its impact on the focus of the investigation.

Of no less importance to the validity and completion of this study were the objectivity, encouragement, and assistance of Florence Breen, Director, Planning and Programming Division, Georgia Department of Transportation, who provided the underpinnings and impetus for this research. Special thanks are due him for the intellectual climate as well as the technical support. Additionally, a note of appreciation is in order to John Hassell, former Chief, Policy Planning Office, who offered professional suggestions while channelling pertinent information from the Commissioner's Office and the Georgia Congressional Delegation. Moreover, as the key planning official in the Federal Highway Administration, he offered signal observations that are included herein.

I have been privileged to work with Bill Bivens, Principal Fellow for Rural Policy with the National Governors' Conference. He provided numerous insights and salient comments and shared his conceptualizations, which were adopted, subsequently, by the White House.

Among the many who urged me to focus on rural problems and expand on poverty issues were Dr. Larry Gess and Dr. Ernie Metivier, while we worked together in the Georgia Governor's Office; Dr. David Sweet, Director of the Ohio Economic and Community Development Department, my mentor, who appointed me Field Director for Economic Advancement; and Professor Irving Hand, Transportation Research Board, who turned me away from several deadends.

Additionally, I am grateful for an early direction toward worker/commuter diseconomies by my major professors at Ohio State University, Professor Glenn Miller, Manpower Economics, and Dr. Jimmie Heskett, Transportation and Logistics; and at Xavier University, Dean Tom Hailstones who taught me the techniques of applied economic analysis.

To all others with whom I interacted in the course of this research but whom I have not mentioned by name, I extend my sincere thanks for their input.

Above all, special and particular thanks, appreciation, gratitude, and love to my dear wife, JoAnn, who endured, advised, encouraged, and adjusted to unreasonable demands, and edited and typed the many drafts, iterations, and modifications throughout. This book would not exist in its present length and form without her expertise, patience, and levity. Her support was priceless.

Thanks also to my son, Joe, for his general good humor and teasing, which helped to mollify the tedium and anxiety of such an exercise.

To be sure, any omissions or errors are my responsibility.

To my lady
JoAnn
who dedicated herself
to my work
to my growth
to my life.

Transportation
for the Poor

1 BACKGROUND

The intent of this study is to examine general relationships among (1) mobility, (2) personal income, and (3) work activity in rural areas. The study is designed to consider the possibility that limited personal mobility impedes access to work activities, which in turn determine personal income. To illustrate these relationships, it includes a case study of residents of some counties in rural Georgia who are economically disadvantaged because their lack of personal mobility limits locations and time intervals in which work activity is accessible. In short, some rural Americans simply do not have the ability to go from home to work to home. The study concludes with a series of policy proposals that will, it is hoped, be useful to other states attempting to solve this important and pressing problem. Terms such as *mobility, personal income,* and *work activity* are defined and explained in detail below.

It should be fully understood that this problem is not new, nor is it addressed solely to rural areas, nor is it limited to the state of Georgia. Rather, the condition can be ascribed mostly to a long history of benign neglect.

Relatively easy access to employment sites plays an important role in employment decisions by job seekers. Where potential job holders and prospective job seekers cannot walk safely to work within fifteen to thirty minutes, other modes of transportation are necessary. Kaye (1976a) defines

1

transportation as the physical means required to move between two points to satisfy the need for mobility. The means include conventional transit, jitney, taxi, or transport provided by neighbors.

In most rural areas of America, job seekers outnumber available jobs, and most of these jobs are not within practical walking distance of the job seekers' homes. Clearly these job seekers suffer mobility disadvantages. The *mobility disadvantaged* are people excluding the elderly and handicapped who depend on means of travel other than self-operated vehicles.

Mobility disadvantage is most prevalent in rural counties containing only communities with five thousand residents or less. Such communities fall within the realm of Toner's (1977) "micropolitan" concept. Toner coined the term *micropolitan* to define those habitations that are typically labeled "rural" or "nonurban" and "nonmetropolitan" areas. Conventional methods for meeting the needs of the rural mobility disadvantaged cannot be applied successfully to the problem of these micropolitan areas. Indeed, the urban experience has created false expectations for the rural condition concerning the mobility-generating potential of public transit. In these rural hinterlands, no "mass" exists to transport (Dickey, 1977).

It is not assumed that the geographical profiles resulting from the mobility model in this study apply to all rural inhabitants, nor can "mass" transportation solve the problem. "There are no masses. There are only individuals" (Hughes, 1965, p. 2). However, inputs to the mobility model have generated relationships between sets of comparative statics that can be used as condition indicators and should be viewed only in that context.

Because of the confusion due to changes in urban definitions by the Census Bureau during the last three decades, as well as the apparent disregard for elements other than density and boundary that comprise a community (Coates and Weiss, 1975), it was felt that a more discriminating approach should be taken to define "small" and "rural" communities. The criteria are vague and span at least three quarters of this century (DeJong and Sell, 1977). For instance, demonstration projects under Section 147 of the 1973 Federal-Aid Highway Act and Section 106 of the 1973 Rural Development Act include "places" containing "urbanized areas" ranging from 5,500 to 50,000 inhabitants in their definition of "rural population." "Rural counties" also are defined differently in the methodology section for this research. In some cases exceptions emerge that contradict the "flexible" definition (Maggied, 1979, p. 73). Further, although the census typically classifies places housing over 2,500 inhabitants as urban, DeJong and Sell refer to isolated places with populations between 2,500 and 50,000 as urban but not metropolitan; thus they contain the same population dynamics as rural areas. Similarly, Tarver (1973) investigated changes in southern nonmetropolitan towns that housed between 2,500 and 9,999 inhabitants and reported his findings in a rural publication.

The census definition notwithstanding, Dillman and Tremblay (1977) assert that ruralness connotes various images to different people. Thus the definition for *rural* established in this investigation is believed to be more meaningful than the traditional census definition. Although unincorporated areas are predominantly rural in the country at large, they cannot be equated totally with "rural areas," because they include many densely populated areas, such as urban towns, townships, and counties (including DeKalb, Georgia) around the country. Their lower population density and inadequate public transportation facilities, however, make them functionally more comparable to rural than to urban areas for the transportation planning process. To better deal with population dispersion, class intervals for places were established as indicators that can be used to determine some degree of transportation disadvantage in particular population clusters.

Six class intervals were established to delimit the state under two major urban and rural categories equating to places defined by the U.S. Bureau of Census as 1,000 persons per square mile. Under the rural definition for this research, intervals were set from 2,500 to 4,999 persons, 1,000 to 2,499 persons, and less than 1,000 persons. All areas called "places" by the census refer to incorporated places in the state of Georgia. The residual space beyond these interstices of the incorporated places is what the census refers to as "unincorporated places."

This study focuses on counties with only small communities and attempts to identify the number of rural residents who are mobility disadvantaged and who, as a result, do not obtain employment and thus remain economically deficient as well as mobility disadvantaged. It also attempts to show why conventional methods and paratransit innovated for solving the transportation problem of the rural elderly and handicapped in larger areas cannot succeed in sparsely populated areas. For example, Dial-a-Ride (taxi) door to door requires preset reservations with one to seven days' notice; Hail-a-Ride (jitney) requires some form of transit between the household and the pickup point, which is often unsafe, untimely, cumbersome, and inconvenient. Several other conditions hinder the myriad administrative units that govern these small areas and, subsequently, constrain paratransit and other transportation services.

Ornati (1969) captures the nescience of the journey-to-work problem. Although he focuses on major metropolitan areas, particularly New York City, his assessment of the relationships between transportation deficiencies and economically disadvantaged people is no less significant for rural areas, as noted by Falcocchio and Cantilli (1974):

What it is that makes nonworkers of many of the poor overlaps with other problems of the poor. The problem of getting to where the jobs are (whether the problem is due to poor transportation or because the poor live in ghettos) is part of the larger problem of the lack of mobility of the poor. The social benefits of high labor mobility have been recognized since Adam Smith, in the *Wealth of Nations*, inveighed against "whatever obstructs the free circulation of labour from one employment to another." Yet in spite of a large literature on labor mobility, the physical problem of getting to work does not seem to have been considered until the McCone Commission on the Watts Riot ascribed as a cause of the riots the difficulties that Watts-area residents had in going to work. [Ornati, 1969, pp. vii–viii]

While unemployment rates provide an indicator for the share of people in the labor market who are actively seeking work, these indicators do not reveal the share of the working-age population, defined by the U.S. Bureau of Labor Statistics, who are "nonworkers" and are not included in the labor force. It is believed, moreover, that Ornati's assumption of "nonworker" permits better clarification of the employment/unemployment problem than does the unemployment rate measure reported monthly by the Bureau of Labor Statistics (BLS).

Bureau Commissioner Shishkin (1976) argues, however, that several indicators, including the unemployment rate as well as the employment/population ratio (labor force participation rate), gross national product, and consumer price index, should be used as measures of work activity. At the national level these measures are relatively credible; at county and local levels they are spurious because of the lack of a critical mass. Ornati's assumption suggests that factors other than "job availability" enhance or constrain employment (Maggied, 1979, p. 5). A major factor is mobility. Job availability in small communities and rural areas is nearly impossible to quantify. Consequently, no sound basis for developing an accurate data set for rural job availability could be established.

Although few generalizations can be ascribed to deployment of a labor force, usually it is a function of concentrated population in near proximity to economic growth. One tendency, however, emerges over others: urbanization (Brown, 1962). This proximate concentration allows workers to choose (to some degree) what jobs they prefer among those within their reach. Moreover, they have no intention of leaving their areas (Reynolds, 1951).

In essence, the "effective distances to work activity vary with factors other than distance in miles traveled as the limiter" (Brown, 1962, p. 97). In rural areas, particularly, few jobs are within reach; thus limiting factors other than distance — such as *time, cost,* and *inconvenience* — severely hamper access to the labor market. The limiting time factor suggests a "time hinterland" that plays an important role in what the work commuter considers an acceptable time frame for traveling to a job. The time hinterland concept for commodity movements was idealized during a containerization study for the port of Cleveland, Ohio (Sweet and Maggied, 1967).

Natural barriers, such as streams that are not bridged, impede access to activities "just across the creek." Many such situations prevail in the rural hinterlands of Georgia, particularly in the Appalachian Mountains and Coastal Plains (Lamb, 1975–1979).

By private car, trips over extremely hazardous roads generally require a minimum of ninety minutes — a long time indeed to sit in a vehicle driving to work. Hence distance is not the only important factor when considering transportation needs. The amount of time in commuter transit, coupled with its satisfactions and pleasantries or discomforts, significantly affects whether the transportation service — private or public — will be utilized. A signal point to be made here, however, is that the assumption by Wheeler (1974) of a choice between either migration or commutation nowhere mentions a third option: exit from the labor force. That is, a person might choose to allow reportable weekly benefits to deplete without securing new employment and to discontinue seeking work actively as per the BLS definition; in short, the choice might be resignation to poverty and public assistance.

Thus, the mobility disadvantaged often settle into jobs nearby that are known to them and, therefore, tolerable so long as increasing wage levels do not surpass them.

When urban wage levels increase elsewhere, states Brown (1962), the urban worker often has the option to move. In the rural setting, however, the condition of the "man market," as Brown describes the situation, prevails and provides applicants little chance to play off one employer's offer against another. This lack of opportunity for employee bargaining stems in part, notes Reynolds (1951), from imperfect and partial knowledge; generally it is vague and fragmentary, and the remote worker often is beyond communication linkages to what might be called a market. Even the "typical worker" has no sensation of being in a labor market (Reynolds, 1951) and subsequently suffers from diseconomies in a rising market.

The geographic size of the state, the long distances between urban-industrial areas, and the concomitant size of the rural portion make Georgia an appropriate subject for this type of study. To extend the list of caveats further, it is freely admitted that economically disadvantaged people are found in nonrural places as well. The unemployment rate among inner-city residents offers substantial evidence of this fact. But the transportation difficulties of inner-city residents is a problem far beyond the scope of this study and, it should be pointed out, there are governmental policies and programs designed to alleviate urban transportation ills. The same cannot be said for the vast rural problem.

This research deals with Georgia specifically, but only as a typical state for a case study. The methodology may be applied, therefore, to several states with similar socioeconomic and geopolitical profiles that have developed subregions of several counties each, or to the counties themselves. Although Georgia is not unique, the exact methodology may not be apropos for generalization to permit exact replication in every case, even though working poor pervade most rural areas of the nation. Nonetheless, Georgia's three dissimilar terrain characteristics — Appalachia, Piedmont, and Coastal Plain — provide the opportunity to examine areas in many other states with similar geographic and demographic characteristics that may impinge upon work-trip commuting in privately owned automobiles or public transit operations.

Thus we have a study that uses existing data of an aggregate nature to (1) discuss economic conditions in rural America, (2) demonstrate a relationship between those economic conditions and the mobility of its inhabitants, and (3) examine the strengths and weaknesses of alternative policies and / or programs that might solve this problem.

WHY THIS STUDY NOW?

An unpleasant fact of life known by most workers regardless of where they live is that the cost of getting to and from work by private automobile is rapidly increasing. In a study by Hertz Rent-a-Car, reported in *Popular Science* ("Detroit Report," 1976), two indicators illustrate the seriousness of the problem: (1) the expense of owning and running an automobile increased by 27% during 1974, and (2) the rise in vehicle costs was more than twice the rise in the cost of living during the 1972–1975 period. Based on this report and ancillary information, the typical American spends approximately $4.30 for his or her work trip by automobile, given a single occupant per car. These costs are calculated on the basis of Hertz's 23¢ per mile for the average 18.8 miles traveled to and from work each day (Maggied, 1979, p. 10). Consequently, workers earning $8,000 per year — approximately $31 per day — spend 14% of their gross personal earned income for work trips. This $8,000 level corresponds to the value used by *Sales and Marketing Management* magazine to delimit low-income families. The federal Department of Health, Education, and Welfare redefined the upper-level value for "poverty families" at $9,000 per year in 1978 (Threlkeld, 1978). In unincorporated areas, assumed to be primarily rural, the share of personal earnings used for work transits is even higher: average trip lengths exceed 22 miles per round trip (Svercl and Asin, 1973).

A more extensive study for the U.S. Transportation Department posits that the share of income for transportation costs is more severe in many disadvantaged small communities. Coates (1974) suggests that expenses for transportation may approach 50% of family income. Furthermore, although transportation service is not the most critical ingredient, service within and around small towns is fraught with inadequate, inconvenient, and expensive service. Coates affirms the obvious, that most small-town inhabitants almost totally depend on automobiles for personal travel. More important, however, she asserts that changes from a five-day to a four-day work week could have significant effects on the type of transportation services available for small towns.

Further increases in transportation costs may result in changes in the work status of the rural poor. For if transportation costs for rural families continue to rise significantly without commensurate increases in earned income, the incidence and duration of underemployment, unemployment, and nonemployment may rise substantially. It is expected that automobile operating costs will increase over the next three years at the same rate in relation to the rise in the cost of living as has occurred for these indicators during the 1972–1975 triennium. Should this rise occur, it is posited that rural workers without alternative modes of transportation will (a) opt for lower-paying jobs in closer proximity to their current residence; (b) relocate their dwelling place, enduring the one-time fixed transit cost; or (c) totally withdraw from labor market activity. It is further suggested that although some of the employed poor may select alternatives (a) and/or (b), they are more likely to choose alternative (c) simply because of their economic condition. The budgetary expense to a worker for transportation to a job is as much a cost of doing business as any shipping or delivery expense to a manufacturer, tradesman, or mechanic. In Sirageldin's study (1969), the assumption was made that the journey to work is a pure work activity. Consequently, they concluded that hourly earnings must be computed by including the time spent commuting to and from work.

Assuredly, many other considerations — demographic, social, and ecologic — may impinge upon the choice of the rural resident facing a changing employment market, but this study focuses primarily on the economic aspects of available transportation as a determinant of the employment status of Georgia's rural poor.

In view of the numerous programs at both the federal and state level designed to alleviate the problems of the economically disadvantaged, the additional need to provide transportation services raises several questions.

For example, should state agencies, such as Labor, Community Development, Regional Planning, Policy Analysis, Urban Affairs, or Industry and Trade, develop programs to provide transportation service tailored to their individual programs? Should the authorized regulatory agencies approve requests made by intercity and regional public transportation systems operators for abandonment based only on economics, or should the ridership bear the burden through a variable pricing formula based on the ability to pay for transits? Should the Department of Transportation operate statewide public transportation systems for all employees who reside in rural areas? Should the state inaugurate a "New Volks for Poor Folks" program, as Myers (1968) suggests? These are only a few of the questions that one might consider.

THEORETICAL DEVELOPMENT

Transportation, as an economic resource, is the physical means that is a necessary condition for spatial mobility by persons exchanging their resources — time, skills, and labor — in the market economy of an industrial society (Kaye, 1976b). *Mobility* is the capacity, capability, and opportunity to move. Until recently, decisions affecting the location of industry primarily focused on product processing and distribution costs. While availability of a viable labor force (ample skilled inhabitants) in perceived near proximity was a significant concern, the expense of transporting raw materials from their source to the proposed economic activity and of transporting the subsequent processed goods from the plant to the immediate market was generally the major consideration in the location decision (Hoover, 1948). Criteria for such decisions traditionally have been concerned more with the land (and material) factor's "transfer costs" incurred by procurement and distribution than with the labor factor's mobility or expense and time in personal budget — because land is immobile and humans are not (Hoover, 1948). The "budget" is a plan intended to link human behavior with financial resources (Wildavsky, 1974).

Hoover suggests applying the "massing of reserves" principle to optimize the local labor market just as one would apply it to optimize other internal economies of the firm. Daily commutation is assumed to be limited to relatively short distances. This principle implies that consideration of the labor factor in an economic activity primarily focuses on the large size of the pool residing within commuting distance.

More recently, Stafford (1974) found that several other labor factors have gained prominence and subsequently greater consideration in the location decision. Availability, productivity, and rates of labor score high along with local amenities among decision criteria for underdeveloped (rural) areas. Only "executive convenience" supersedes these labor factors in importance. Such human factors are removed from the traditional academic focus on the classic economic solution. However, they do reflect the importance of personal values as they relate to behaviors that apply to the internal corporate context (members of management) in which location decisions are made. Stafford notes that these factors reveal typically "hidden agendas" of the decisionmaker. But in either decision set — economic or behavioral — neither Hoover nor Stafford considers the expense of time or money incurred by the production worker during the daily work trip. Neither do they consider how the dimension of time interacts with a person's movement through space, particularly in the rural setting. The resource of time, as Gutenschwager (1973) asserts, is included in this study because of its utilitarian effect on personal behavior. Below is a synopsis of premises and principles that underlie the framework of the time hinterland concept mentioned earlier. Each of the experts cited contributed substantially to the development of this theory.

The concept of time is a crucial element as a resource utilized during any work activity. Ellul (1964) asserts that today's work is tied to a clock; workers must obey it and can do nothing about it. Living time, including work and movement, is split and divided into a parcel of disconnected activities. Robbins (1940) postulates that a theory of value applies to human behavior in an exchange economy and is conditioned by the same limitation of means in relation to ends. This relationship itself is a "technical" incident subsumed by the overriding fact of scarcity. He challenges the Ricardian system for stopping at market valuations and not delving further into the behavior of the isolated individual. Unlike Ellul's disconnected activities, Robbins's activities are grouped into two kinds — product and leisure. He posits that the fixed supply of twenty-four hours in the day must be divided between them (Robbins, 1940, pp. 12 and 13). Further, he asserts that life is short and nature is niggardly, but human ends are various; therefore, we must choose. But the scarcity of one's own time and the services of others are equally important. Finally, he affirms that the relationship of an individual's given wants (choice) rather than technical substance (cultural order) is the significant factor in the disposition of an individual's time and resources (Robbins, 1940, p. 22).

Disposition of an individual's time, as Berne (1961) suggests, is not always determined by the individual, but rather is determined by external cultural forces. An individual's time is generally structured to deal with events of external reality. This reality typically is called "work," whether for monetary gain, intellectual pursuit, or social intercourse. Technically, "work" is referred to as an "activity" that provides for recognizing and delimiting work time (including transit time) from other complex forms of social intercourse. The daily problem of the individual revolves around how his or her working hours are structured. Specifically, it assumes the immediate problem of how one structures time most profitably based on one's own, and others', idiosyncracies — and the potentialities of maximizing permissible satisfactions. Berne refers to "programming" as the operational aspects of structuring time. This programming is supplied by three sources: material, social, and individual. Material programming evolves from the seriation of events encountered when dealing with external reality. For this study, Berne's definitions of "social" and "individual" programming do not apply.

Attempting to determine what an individual's satisfactions or wants happen to be is difficult at best. Marshall (1961) posits that when the element of time becomes part of the transaction, quantities of two benefits received at different times cannot be compared; nor can the same value be applied to these benefits for different individuals' satisfaction at the same point in time. Further, he notes the difficulty in ascertaining the proportions of their earned income that individuals in different socioeconomic classes distribute between necessities and other expenditures (Marshall, 1961, p. 115).

Knowledge of an individual's wants regarding *any* option is — if ever available — seldom discernible. Skinner (1953) refers to this as the psychic link, or inner condition, in a causal chain consisting of three links. The other two include (a) an operation performed on the organism from without and (b) a kind of behavior. He postulates that if the inner condition were known, behavior may be predictable without information about the original operation. But he also argues that the practice of looking inside the organism for an explanation of behavior often supplies spurious answers. Furthermore, such answers tend to obscure variables that are immediately available for scientific analyses. Skinner suggests, moreover, that inner states are not relevant in a functional analysis; additionally, the observer cannot account for the behavior of any system while remaining within it. Instead, forces acting upon the organism from without must be observed from beyond the system.

In summary, Skinner concludes that the topography of behavior may be described in a manner that allows given instances to be identified quite accurately by any qualified, detached observer.

This approach of observing human behavior principally is no less valid in the field of economics than it is in the field of psychology. This principle, as Von Neumann and Morgenstern (1953) proffer, applies to the forms of exchanges between a few individuals in the same manner as those observed in major markets of modern industry. This principle also applies to barter exchange between states. While exact proofs may be unattainable, this approach permits treatment of manageable problems that will lead to quantifiable results. Although the results may be intuitively well known, it is necessary to gain as much knowledge as possible about the individual within his or her environment and about the simplest forms of exchange in that environment.

These views were adopted by the founders of the marginal utility school and are extended from the perspective of "games of strategy." This perspective permits formalizing events in a social (market) exchange economy by using a number of variables that describe actions of the participants in this economy. This is not an attempt to treat "rational" economic behavior through, for example, indifference curves any more than there is the need to treat the "inner condition" in psychological behavior. Rather, this "strategies" approach permits empirical control through purely verbal definitions and in no other way. Thus the notion of utility is raised above the level of a tautology where the results of the experimental outcomes can be compared with experience.

The key variables to be used in this study for measuring the parameters of mobility, personal income, and work activity are (1) "carless" incidence, (2) median family income, and (3) labor force participation rates. Other variables such as commutation, place size, density, rurality, speed (time/distance), and unpaved roads are also observed to ascertain whether other phenomena may condition work trips. To be sure, while the unfavorable conditions described by these latter variables heavily influence the statistical profiles of Georgia's rural counties and places, cases have been reported where low-income workers travel relatively long distances to obtain steady work. For example, Wellslager (1978) found that in the early 1970s workers residing in Dougherty County (Albany SMSA), Georgia, traveled more than ninety miles one way to Macon (Bibb County) for steady employment. This study recognizes that such events do occur. But owing to a finite pool of resources and the constraints of time, no attempt has been made to explore the variables beyond the first three detailed above. Several studies have revealed that various factors other than distance or time also impinge upon the decision to work. However, most of the information gathered in those studies has been provided by employers, not by employees.

Observations

Since this study is intended to examine general relationships among (1) mobility, (2) personal income, and (3) work activity in rural areas, it treats the setting of locations and time intervals as a part of these relationships. It investigates how they impede access to work activity, which determines personal revenues and expenses.

Mosely et al. (1977) posit that no rural area is an island; thus no unambiguous way exists to define "rural" areas. Using economic, demographic, geographic, or social criteria results in varying degrees of overlap. They stress three characteristics that identify the rural condition: (1) sparsely populated commuter hinterlands, (2) remote interstices inaccessible to urban systems, and (3) dynamic change in the spatial structure relating to the rural society and economy.

Gould (1969) refers to accessibility as a slippery notion that contains two dimensions: legal/social and physical. This study deals with the latter dimension — that which provides an individual with the material facilities of transportation (cars and roads) needed to reach supply points at suitable times.

The concept of work activity is a complex phenomenon to define. While it is generally reduced to "paid employment," work activity often provides social and psychic income. Also, use of Upjohn's definition of work as "an activity that produces something of value for other people . . ." (*Work in America*, 1973) further complicates the meaning. For example, it excludes the housewife who receives "in-kind" income for her myriad "services," which are considered immeasurable in economic terms. This study, however, will define work activity in measurable economic terms, such as personal income, labor force participation, and/or number employed.

Revenues and *expenses* are terms used in this study for accounting dollar flows rather than *income* and *costs*, because they more readily relate to personal family budget receipts and expenditures within specified time spans. Stigler (in Watson, 1965) asserts that the economic concept of income is complex and basically incapable of precise measurement; he infers that direct comparison of incomes and costs between spatial entities is irrelevant under different conditions. Further, *revenue* is defined by Esser Nemmers (1966) as cash received in a period of time; *expense* is defined as cash outlays incurred in the production of a good or service.

Regardless of where a work activity is situated in relation to a "station" (even within the residence), some form of movement is required. *Station* is defined as a fixed location where a body remains. Thus a *stationary activity* is an exchange of conventionally valued human resources for personal income while present at a fixed location.

This movement or "transit" directly depends on the availability of transportation means to facilitate the transit, whether they be feet to move the body across cleared floors or on stairs between tiers, or wheeled vehicles to propel the object across designated ways between two stations.

Transit is defined as the unit of incidence where a body moves between two or more stations. Thus a *transitionary activity* is an exchange of conventionally valued human resources for personal income while in transit between fixed locations. Little attention has been focused on such transits in rural areas, whether in terms of time or of cost. Studies reviewed either infer or refer directly to urban facilities (Stopher, 1974) and situations (U.S. Department of Transportation, 1974). Even future-oriented studies focus on urban transportation service for communities rather than on the total urban/rural perspective. Suggested improvements by Ward et al. (1977) include scenarios of high-density developments "that are pleasant and convenient places" to live, work, and walk.

Also, a semantic problem intrudes to confuse the rural definition. The label of "small community" connotes an entity that has an infrastructure sufficient to maintain itself but generally is located in nonurban surroundings. Such communities typically are situated in what were defined as economic development regions substantially distant from metropolitan areas. Understandably, most studies dealing with transportation, income, and employment activities are focused on large metropolitan areas housing and serving inhabitants by the hundreds of thousands; but once they are delimited at 50,000 people, as Coates and Weiss (1975) note, the residual cities are labeled "small communities." A vast difference exists between cities containing 500,000 inhabitants and 50,000. But the difference between towns of 50,000 and 5,000 is greater still. And programs applicable to urbanized areas and urban areas over 5,000 are not relevant to rural America's villages of 5,000 inhabitants or fewer, where no critical mass of population occurs. Most nonmetropolitan or small-community transportation activities and programs focus on towns and cities where population exceeds 10,000 inhabitants.

Although 2,500 inhabitants delimits "rural" places, communities containing 5,000 inhabitants substantially removed (fifty miles) from the outer boundaries of counties in urbanized areas cannot be considered self-sustaining and thus are transportation disadvantaged (Kaye, 1977).

Coates and Wiess (1975, p. 1) are among the early few who have recognized that "rural" small towns extend from places containing 1,000 inhabitants to cities containing 25,000. Further, they note that 31% of the American population resides in villages under 1,000 people, while 15% resides in hamlets or other rural settlements too small to be categorized as "places" by the Census Bureau. While their study focuses on eight communities of 5,000 to 10,000 inhabitants, few if any statistics detailing variables and developed by the census or other sources are reported describing communities of 1,000 to 5,000 inhabitants. Under the Bureau of Census guidelines (1970), communi-

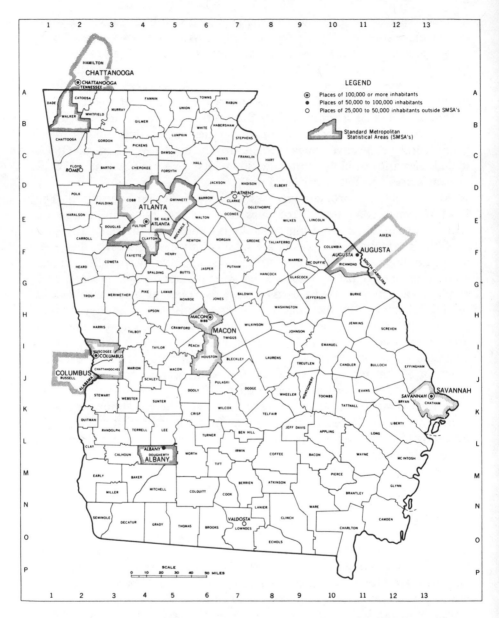

Figure 1.1. Demographic Representation of Urban Places in Georgia: 1970. *Source:* U.S. Department of Commerce, Bureau of Census (1973b, p. 97).

ties containing more than 2,500 inhabitants typically are classified as "urban." "Other urban" are categorized as 10,000 or more, and 2,500 to 10,000; "rural" are categorized as 1,000 to 2,500 and "other rural." Figure 1.1 displays the major population centers in Georgia.

In Georgia, 326 of the 573 incorporated places have less than 1,000 inhabitants, and 168 communities house between 1,000 and 5,000 inhabitants (see Table 1.1). (The United States has 9,515 places with less than 1,000 inhabitants and 7,113 places with 1,000 to 5,000.) Thus it seems likely that the journey to work was a problem for residents in areas more remote from large employment centers. Furthermore, it was believed that lack of mobility in rural areas hampered that journey.

Discussing concepts with proper nomenclature and adequate definitions presents many difficulties when experts apply different terms to mean the same thing. It becomes even more cumbersome when applying the same term to two distinct populations or applying different terms to the same population. In the case of "mobility disadvantaged," semantic problems become quite evident. Throughout the literature search for this study, experts were found who used their own terminology to define concepts that were markedly similar or the same. For example, Kaye (1976b) differentiates between two basic terms: *mobility*, which means the capacity, the capability, and the opportunity to move (Maggied, 1979a, p. 14), and *transportation*, which means only the physical elements of moving — that is, ways of satisfying the need for mobility.

Kaye also considers the problem of distinguishing between *demand* and *need*. He argues that the perceptions of the responsible agencies, some administrators, and professionals that fail to distinguish between need and demand must be challenged. He cites comments in erstwhile Secretary of Agriculture Earl Butz's third annual report to Congress regarding rural development goals (Kaye, 1976b). Butz argued that while transit need is obvious and significant, hinterland demand traditionally has been too low to pay for investment in rural bus service. From the perspective of the Department of Agriculture, demand for rural transportation services is very low. Kaye (1976b) counters their arguments about demand for service occurring only when someone is willing to pay for it. By this reasoning, he submits that demand for substandard housing is high and for social security low. Thus transit fare box revenues may not be the best indicator of demand.

Findings in other studies corroborate the notion that mobility, personal income, and work activity maintain a symbiotic relationship. Even the classic sociological study, *Talley's Corner* (Liebow, 1967), only skirts the problem. The section opens with the following setting:

Table 1.1. Number of Incorporated Places in Georgia and Its Area Planning and Development Commission Regions: Mid-1975

	Number of Incorporated Places by Place-Size Interval						
	0–999 Pop.	1,000–2,499 Pop.	2,500–4,999 Pop.	5,000–9,999 Pop.	10,000–24,999 Pop.	25,000–49,999 Pop.	Over 50,000 Pop.
United States	9,515	4,818	2,295	1,839	1,385	520	396
Georgia	326	99	69	37	29	7	6
Altamaha Southern	14	1	6	1	2	0	0
Atlanta Metropolitan	10	4	12	12	7	3	1
Central Savannah	28	7	5	3	0	0	1
Chattahoochee-Flint	19	6	4	0	3	0	0
Coastal Crescent	7	11	2	2	1	0	1
South Georgia	15	4	5	1	1	1	0
Coosa Valley	18	7	5	5	1	1	0
Georgia Mountains	33	6	4	1	1	0	0
Heart of Georgia	28	4	5	1	1	0	0
Lower Chattahoochee	14	6	1	0	0	0	1
McIntosh Trail	19	4	5	0	3	0	0
Middle Flint	11	7	2	0	2	0	0
Middle Georgia	6	4	1	2	0	1	1
Northeast Georgia	38	5	2	4	0	1	0
North Georgia	15	6	2	0	1	0	0
Oconee Valley	15	4	2	1	1	0	0
Southeast Georgia	6	6	3	0	2	0	0
Southwest Georgia	30	7	3	4	3	0	1

Source: Derived estimates from U.S. Department of Commerce, Bureau of Census (1977a).

A pickup drives slowly down the street. The truck stops as it comes abreast of a man sitting on a cast-iron porch and the white driver calls out, asking if the man wants a day's work. The man shakes his head and the truck moves on up the block, stopping again whenever idling men come within calling distance of the driver. At the Carryout corner, five men debate the question briefly and shake their heads *no* to the truck. The truck turns the corner and repeats the same performance up the next street. In the distance, one can see one man, then another, climb into the back of the truck and sit down. In starts and stops, the truck finally disappears.

What is it we have witnessed here? A labor scavenger rebuffed by his would-be prey? Lazy, irresponsible men turning down an honest day's pay for an honest day's work? *Or a more complex phenomenon marking the intersection of economic forces, social values, and individual states of mind and body?* [Liebow, 1967, pp. 291–30; italics added]

While Liebow only briefly touches on the accessibility problem, his description of the street corner scene and the scenario of the white truck driver's mindset — which conflicts with his actions of trolling the streets with full intention of attracting some day laborers — points to generalizations and misconceptions. It also suggests, as Eyestone (1972) professes, a callousness concerning the physical discomfort that employers, officials, and the public in general believe that the poor should endure when traveling to and from work.

Job competition is always fierce. Liebow's example of the particular jobs available to the poor points to the insensitivity and unawareness that often prevail concerning public transportation. Liebow was one of the first to recognize that both getting construction jobs in outlying areas and getting to them are relatively more difficult than is the case for continual, menial jobs in retailing and the service trades in central, stationary locations. Furthermore, urban poverty housing paradoxically rests on the most expensive land in the city. The poor live on these lands in order to obtain short-time travel to work (Wheeler, 1974). In their plight of high-cost housing, poor families cannot afford the luxury of high-level mobility. Moreover, little effort has been focused on the identification of families suffering such inaccessibility. No data were discovered in the area of cross-classifying socioeconomic variables, particularly family income and automobile ownership. Unfortunately, Byrne and Neumann (no date) discovered that such cross tabulations are unavailable in the census, even at the enumeration district level. Apparently these cross tabulations will not be forthcoming in the 1980 census publications despite repeated requests by potential users (Fulton, 1978). It is disconcerting to note that after due deliberation about this datum, it will be omitted intentionally. Rural nonfarm households, however, represent a unique combination of four basic factors, including income level and mobility preferences, in which relative housing costs are considered a constant in their decision rules regarding housing choices (Wheeler, 1974). Therefore, distance to the employment center, measured in travel costs and effort, is a paramount factor. Only those families that are unusually mobile (high personal income with several cars) are willing to substitute the inconvenience of daily long-distance commuting for savings in housing costs associated with the rural environment. The very poorest families, therefore, cannot afford the substitution and live close to work.

In contrast to low-income urban poor, low-income ruralites incur relatively cheap housing costs, since land is plentiful and demand by industry is relatively low. But generally little mobility prevails for the poor (See Table 1.2). Thus access to jobs is impeded either, as Batchelder (1966) argues, because no transit facilities or systems exist or because transportation costs are relatively high. The U.S. Department of Transportation states that while over 80% of rural households own at least one automobile, the public transportation system in rural America is inadequate; it does not fill the gap of 20% left by the private automobile. Taxi systems, where they exist, are expensive. Jitneys are scarce because they, also, are unprofitable. Rail and bus services predominate only between major urban areas. They do not adequately serve most rural areas or rural residents (U.S. Department of Transportation, 1977a). More important, it is quite evident that intercity bus service does not operate off the numbered highways or on the byways designated as county roads. *Byway* refers to roads that are not included in the federal and state network. In many counties a large percentage of byways is unpaved. Wheeler (1974) reports that such lack of carrier service, coupled with the unimproved road conditions reported by USDOT (see Table 1.3), leaves few alternatives other than migration or private automobile commutation.

In some respects, Wheeler overlooks a significant element in the journey-to-work pattern. Some industries and topography do not lend themselves to other than long-distance commutation. For example, in the coal fields of mountainous West Virginia, Kentucky, and Virginia — a one-industry area — the terrain is so rugged and steep that housing for miners cannot be located near the workplace. Considering needs for industry, commerce, and infrastructure, the contour provides little land for residential housing. In one report, community leaders stated that it was not uncommon for workers to travel fifty miles one way over less than adequate highways and byways (Maggied, 1979, p. 39). A more recent study by Kaye (1977) substantiated that workers will commute almost sixty miles one way to obtain employment. An industrial plant study for a rural county in Illinois revealed that the commuting field was fifty-seven miles; additionally, more than 8% of the employees traveled over twenty miles to work (Maggied, 1979, p. 40).

Table 1.2. Selected Demographic Mobility Characteristics for Georgia and Its APDCs: 1970

Area	Rural Population as Percent of Total Area	Occupied Rural Households as Percent of Total Households	Rural Households as Percent of Total Households	
			Without Cars	Without Phones
United States	26.5%	25.0%	11.7%	18.0%
Georgia	39.7	38.1	14.1	27.1
Altamaha Southern	56.4	52.8	14.6	32.8
Atlanta Metropolitan	15.5	14.5	5.9	10.6
Central Savannah River	41.0	40.1	19.3	33.7
Chattahoochee Flint	56.9	55.3	15.5	25.8
Coastal Crescent	28.7	27.3	13.9	26.7
South Georgia	51.0	49.1	14.0	33.4
Coosa Valley	63.4	61.4	11.4	23.1
Georgia Mountains	82.9	82.4	12.8	26.6
Heart of Georgia	65.3	63.8	19.3	36.0
Lower Chattahoochee	19.4	17.3	26.0	37.5
McIntosh Trail	64.3	61.8	13.1	24.1
Middle Flint	64.4	62.7	22.7	38.0
Middle Georgia	29.7	27.0	13.8	27.3
North Georgia	82.8	79.5	11.8	28.9
Northeast Georgia	61.5	60.4	14.3	26.0
Oconee Valley	59.0	63.5	21.3	36.8
Southeast Georgia	57.6	54.7	14.5	33.0
Southwest Georgia	45.6	43.9	18.4	33.4

Source: Derived estimates from U.S. Department of Commerce, Bureau of Census (1973c, Pt. 12, Table 62, pp. 12-100, 12-224–263).

19

Table 1.3. Population Density and Percent of Unpaved County Roads in Georgia and Its APDCs: 1976–1977

Area	Area Density, 1977*	Percent Unpaved County Roads, 1977	Percent Black Inhabitants, 1976
United States	61	22.6%	13.2%
Georgia	86	57.0	26.4
Altamaha Southern	29	79.2	27.5
Atlanta Metropolitan	771	20.0	22.1
Central Savannah	58	62.8	36.1
Chattahoochee Flint	75	45.7	28.0
Coastal Crescent	79	58.2	32.2
South Georgia	49	70.7	29.3
Coosa Valley	99	35.7	8.8
Georgia Mountains	64	53.4	7.8
Heart of Georgia	31	72.0	30.4
Lower Chattahoochee	83	56.8	32.1
McIntosh Trail	110	47.1	28.7
Middle Flint	33	65.9	46.9
Middle Georgia	121	56.7	32.5
Northeast Georgia	73	52.5	24.5
North Georgia	72	44.1	2.7
Oconee Valley	32	66.3	47.7
Southeast Georgia	24	78.4	22.6
Southwest Georgia	50	66.4	38.0

Source: Derived estimates from "The Survey of Buying Power Data Service, 1977" (1978) and U.S. Department of Transportation, Planning Data Services Section (1977c).
*Number of inhabitants per square mile.

The same problem of labor choices is discussed in the urban context by Falcocchio and Cantilli (1974) with respect to the Bedford-Stuyvesant ghetto in Brooklyn, New York. There, too, near total dependency on the private automobile for personal transportation resulted in the decline of transit service. This decline has shut out the poor from work opportunities in Bedford-Stuyvesant; additionally, the poor service has been a major factor in the decline of public transit patronage practically everywhere in the country, particularly because of the emotional as well as economic dependence on the private automobile. Moreover, for a substantial portion of the working population, commuting across county lines in the journey to work appears to be significant in several regions of Georgia (see Table 1.4 and Figure 1.2). A detailed analysis on place of work by the Bureau of the Census (U.S. Department of Commerce, 1970b) indicates that these conditions do not prevail in most states outside the northeast quadrant of the United States. A more recent, cursory review by Bowles and Beale (1980) suggests that southern workers commute intercounty more so than the rest of the United States.

Wilfred Owen, in his *Accessible City*, discusses the conflict that transportation has brought to the city along with its benefits. He notes that in the 1960s the nation gained 23 million people but also added 31 million more vehicles. Thus the machine was outstripping the human being. In the metropolitan and suburban areas, home-to-work commuting automobiles characteristically carried 80% of the work force.

Owen (1972) reported that transportation (as the fourth expenditure item) commanded almost 13% of consumer expenditures, most of it for automobiles. People spent more for cars than for clothing, and nearly twice as much for transportation services as for medical services. Further, he reported that financial and psychological, as well as physical, factors created preferences for the automobile over public transit.

The fixed costs of insurance and maintenance and the ubiquitous monthly automobile payment are ever present despite any operating economies motorists might attempt to impose upon themselves. The near threefold increase in fuel costs over the last six years appears to have had little impact on total demand. Additionally, Owen (1972) assumes, with others, that price, high taxes, congestion, and restrictive policies have little impact on demand for the private automobile.

A signal point must be presented here. Dependence on the automobile in the city or in the country is due to more than ownership or lack of public transit. While it is a matter of personal preference, convenience, and individual economics as perceived by the user, Owen states:

Table 1.4. Selected Socioeconomic Characteristics for Georgia and Its APDCs: 1969-1971

Area	Percent Out-County Commuters, 1970	Percent Families under 125% Poverty Level, 1969	Percent Households Receiving Aid to Families with Dependent Children, 1971
United States	19.2%	15.0%	20.6%
Georgia	26.8	22.5	27.3
Altamaha Southern	13.9	34.4	6.6
Atlanta Metropolitan	39.7	12.8	6.0
Central Savannah	17.3	29.2	11.1
Chattahoochee Flint	20.5	25.7	7.0
Coastal Crescent	8.4	23.8	9.0
South Georgia	12.2	32.5	7.0
Coosa Valley	29.7	19.7	4.3
Georgia Mountains	21.3	25.6	3.2
Heart of Georgia	23.2	36.3	7.7

Table 1.4. Selected Socioeconomic Characteristics for Georgia and Its APDCs: 1969–1971 (Continued)

Area	Percent Out-County Commuters, 1970	Percent Families under 125% Poverty Level, 1969	Percent Households Receiving Aid to Families with Dependent Children, 1971
Lower Chattahoochee	31.9	26.4	8.6
McIntosh Trail	33.4	22.1	6.6
Middle Flint	17.3	37.8	13.8
Middle Georgia	19.4	22.6	8.0
Northeast Georgia	25.5	24.9	5.6
North Georgia	23.5	20.7	2.9
Oconee Valley	18.6	34.1	11.2
Southeast Georgia	12.1	32.7	8.0
Southwest Georgia	12.2	34.1	9.5

Source: Derived estimates from U.S. Department of Commerce, Bureau of Census (1978a, Table 2, pp. 93, 105, 117; 1978b) and Georgia Department of Human Resources, Division of Family and Children Services Statistical Unit (1977a).

Figure 1.2. Growth Areas and Growth Corridors in Georgia: 1977. *Source:* Georgia Department of Community Affairs, Community Development Division (1981).

24

The reason for preferring private over public transit is not, as often alleged, the perversity of the consumer or his ignorance of economics. Part of the reason can be ascribed to the public policy that has favored the car, but the basic reason why most urban trips are made by automobiles is that the family car, despite its shortcomings, is *superior to any other method of transportation*. It offers comfort, privacy, limited walking, minimum waiting, and freedom from schedules or routing. It guarantees a seat; carries extra passengers at no extra cost; and for most trips, except those in the center city, gets there faster and cheaper than any other way. The transit rider confronts an entirely different situation. He must walk, wait, stand, and be exposed to the elements. The ride is apt to be costly, slow, and uncomfortable because of antiquated equipment, poor ventilation, and service that is congested in rush hours, infrequent during any other time of day, inoperative at night, and nonexistent in suburbia.

The automobile is also a highly versatile method of movement that serves commuter, social, recreational, and business travel needs alike. . . . It is easy to make a choice between car and public carrier on the basis of the service rendered and the costs that have to be paid. On a service basis the automobile generally wins out on time savings alone. . . . When it comes to cost, the amount that people pay to drive depends on whether their car is large or small, new or used. . . . to a driver making a short trip the *perceived* cost may be zero. [Owen, 1976, pp. 5–7; italics added]

This transit decline has been recognized to some degree by policy analysts in their efforts to devise a program for job development (Ferman, 1969). The program would include development of a transportation system to ensure mobility from workers' residences to places of employment. Ferman cites, among three factors as requirements for job development in rural areas, geographic mobility to centers of employment both within and outside Appalachia. Nowhere, however, does he mention how to travel.

Accessibility: Mobility plus Transportation

In reference to accessibility, it is striking that lack of transportation for the poor was not considered a major factor in joblessness. *Accessibility* is defined in this research as the ability of a person to reach a desired activity in another location. It is even more striking that the seeming "indifference" by the poor as perceived by the nonpoor has not been recognized by manpower authorities and labor experts as, perhaps, not indifference at all but rather resignation to an unsatisfactory and cumbersome transportation arrangement.

Traditionally, fixed routes determined by rail or trolley wires (with vehicles adhering to rigid schedules) threaded the white-dominated urban

Table 1.5 Labor Force Participation and Household Income in Georgia and Its APDCs: 1974-1976

Area	Labor Force Participation, 1976	Number of Area Households, 1976	Median Family/Household Income, 1976	% Households Earning under $8,000 Annually, 1974
United States	61.8%	74,002.4	$13,781	32%
Georgia	61.5	1,622.4	$12,363	41
Altamaha Southern	61.3	41.3	9,380	51
Atlanta Metropolitan	67.9	547.3	14,827	40
Central Savannah	54.5	93.3	8,486	45
Chattahoochee Flint	62.8	52.6	10,306	44
Coastal Crescent	53.8	95.9	11,101	41
South Georgia	57.7	55.1	8,513	51
Coosa Valley	61.4	112.9	11,736	38
Georgia Mountains	61.1	71.4	10,275	43
Heart of Georgia	59.8	34.7	7,593	57
Lower Chattahoochee	48.9	69.3	8,671	40
McIntosh Trail	62.6	57.5	12,284	40
Middle Flint	59.5	28.0	7,546	51
Middle Georgia	57.4	87.7	11,762	39
Northeast Georgia	62.3	71.4	10,384	44
North Georgia	65.8	49.9	11,173	36
Oconee Valley	56.2	25.6	9,674	49
Southeast Georgia	56.3	33.7	8,742	51
Southwest Georgia	57.8	94.8	7,967	49

Source: Derived estimates (APDC values were mean averaged using precalculated county medians) from Georgia Department of Labor, Division of Research and Statistics (1977b); U.S. Department of Labor, Bureau of Labor Statistics (1977); Georgia Office of Planning and Budget, Management Review Division (1977–1978); and "The Survey of Buying Power Data Service, 1977" (1978).

thoroughfares and affluent-oriented interurban highways. Such public transit routes were oriented to the middle class in nonpoor neighborhoods. Ornati (1969, pp. 47–55) discovered that even after the changeover to more flexible motor buses with extensions, routes and schedules remained essentially the same despite residential and employment dispersal. Such inflexible transport systems do not fulfill the need of the worker transiting in remote areas whose work schedule may differ sharply from the transit system's working hours.

This problem is substantially more significant in rural areas, and little is or can be done to alleviate the situation. The crux of the problem is that the unfilled jobs are located where the employed are not, and no cost-effective public transit mechanisms exist to level these imbalances. A brief look at differences in labor force levels in Georgia for specified areas (see Table 1.5) suggests that employment opportunities are indeed not equal.

The problem is adequately summarized, despite the focus on urbanites, by Meyer and Kain (1968). They assert that low-income workers are increasingly forced to choose between (a) a higher-paying job that is inaccessible by public transit and thus requires them to pay more for transportation by purchasing and operating their own automobile, and (b) a lower-paying job that is served by transit. Frequently, neither job will be attractive enough to induce nonemployed workers to invest money or time from their meager budgets to become employed.

It is interesting to note that these unbalanced conditions to which Falcocchio and Cantilli, Meyer and Kain, Liebow, Ornati, and others refer are located in the northeast quadrant of the country or in large, compact urban areas where the transit system is fixed, in place, and already "efficiently" operating. They refer to regions where employment is relatively high and where public transit costs to the user are extremely low.

While all these conditions (except for household densities describing poor central-city dwellers and ghetto blacks) pertain to the rural poor, nowhere throughout the 1968 Conference on Poverty and Transportation do the discussants allude to the poverty problem as it relates to rural transportation systems. In summary, we believe that *the mobility/personal income/work activity relationship is a circular phenomenon*. The model explicated below describes this phenomenon, and the subsequent research design establishes a framework to test this belief.

A Theoretical Model

A person can expend part of a finite lifetime and use other available resources when changing from one location to another within a finite range of physical space. The part of the person's lifetime expended and the other available resources used determine the economic value of each such movement, or *transit*. Correspondingly, a person can expend part of a lifetime and use other available resources while occupying a single location. The part of the person's lifetime expended and the other available resources used determine the economic value of each such occupancy, or *station*.

Many questions arise when addressing the problem of people traveling to and from work. While income levels would seem to determine distance traveled, time spent, and transit used by persons traveling to and from the workplace, findings in the *Nationwide Personal Transportation Study* (Svercl and Asin, 1973) reveal that some high-salary people purchase relatively low-cost public transportation while, conversely, some relatively low-salary people purchase high-cost private transportation. It follows that their criterion for accessing employment opportunities is not solely a function of transit cost but, rather, some other factor. A corollary may operate here. However, personal income *may* determine job mobility. Additionally, distance traveled and time spent vary greatly among individual income classes. The salient point about the conceptual framework of this model must be stated here. The model represents my own perception of causal relationships. "Facts do not speak for themselves; we select the facts we want from a universe of them" (Hughes, 1965, p. iv).

Rational solutions to these differences are complex; they involve psychological factors that, to be interpreted, would require an excursion into conditions of utility that is not the intent of this study. Instead, this research focuses on the economic feasibility of persons or families who are unable to acquire transportation in the marketplace. Feasibility in this study partly reflects effective demand, an underlying condition for determining whether some members of some income classes in rural America suffer a mobility disadvantage. To establish whether effective demand plays a role in relative disadvantage, a feasible rate of expenditures for transits was developed to measure the incidence of that disadvantage. To demonstrate how a consistent set of measurements can be assured for each defined geographic region, this model was developed to identify resources for personal mobility as they operate in a market economy. The fundamental concept is described below.

Personal Mobility in a Market Economy. Personal mobility is a basic, time-invariant factor of personal revenues and expenses in a market economy. The primary unit of incidence of revenue and expense in this basic object (of the personal mobility factor) is the *transit*. Because it is a relatively scarce object of the personal mobility factor, its representation is a primary, time-invariant object class in the personal mobility budget. The secondary classes, or subclasses, of the budget are the representations of the various distinct kinds of transitionary space modules. The number of subclasses is a function of the number of distinct stations (locations) in the market at which personal demand is potentially or actually effective in the exchanges of personal revenues and expenses. The value of each budget object subclass is the *feasible rate of expenditure* of transits in transitionary space modules of the kind represented by the subclass. The feasible rate of expenditure is a function of the *expected rate of personal income* and *feasible effective personal demand*.

This budget is not an intensive budget but rather an extensive budget that assumes an instantaneous rate — that is, a snapshot of a point in time dealing with comparative statics. The basic parameters are personal in nature; they deal with (a) personal time, (b) personal space, (c) personal income, and (d) personal market activity.

The key criterion used for weighing the extent of the disadvantaged was the comparison of data that describe Georgia, its counties, and its substate regions against data that describe the country. The design of the substate regions comports to the eighteen Area Planning and Development commissions (APDCs) as they are designated currently (see Figure 1.3). Data previously published at this geopolitical level were used wherever practicable. When such data did not exist, available county data were aggregated to the regional level. In cases where aggregate regional analysis, or comparison to the country, was meaningless, other procedures were used. Such cases are described more fully in subsequent chapters. Selected variables used as the data base were extracted primarily from the U.S. Bureau of Census, the U.S. Bureau of Labor Statistics, the U.S. Federal Highway Administration, and "Survey of Buying Power" publications.

Generally, 1970 data served as the base year. Whenever possible, data from updated reports were used to complement census-year data. Variables developed by the Georgia Data Center also were used, as were other data sources such as university research center publications. Equally important, experts in the field of transportation throughout the nation who deal with the problem of the mobility disadvantaged were contacted often. These contacts included officials from the U.S. Urban Mass Transportation Administration, the Federal Highway Administration, the National Association of Counties Research Foundation, the Institute of Public Administration, the National Transit Association, and many state transportation institutes and departments, among other research organizations. From these contacts a comprehensive library of literature was assembled and reviewed. Following exploration of these sources, the following variables were selected:

Figure 1.3. Designation of Geographic Limits for the Georgia Area Planning and Development Commissions: 1979.

1. Geographic delineation for distances (1972) — urban, commuter, and nonurban (U, C, N);
2. Percent of families who are carless (1970);
3. Labor force participation rates as a percent of population 16 years of age and older (1976);
4. Annual median family income (1976);
5. Percent of resident workers as intercounty commuters (1970);
6. Number of communities under 5,000 population (1975);
7. Rural inhabitants as a percent of total population (1976);
8. Population/land-area density ratio (1976);
9. Percent of unpaved county roads (1976);
10. Percent of families who are phoneless (1970);
11. Percent of total families in poverty (1970);
12. Percent of total families earning $8,000 or less per year (1976);
13. Percent of labor force unemployed;
14. Median years education of adult population 25 years of age and older;
15. Percent of total families receiving Aid to Families with Dependent Children (1971);
16. Black inhabitants as a percent of total population (1976);
17. Intercounty time/distance ratio matrix (1972);
18. Cost of travel as percent of family income (1976).

The choice of the variables provides a basis for developing a profile that describes to some degree the residents and their environs in rural Georgia. In this case, the profile is a composite of conditions describing Georgia's mobility-disadvantaged inhabitants. Where available, rural data were extracted to more adequately describe the target population. Although the illustrations will display information describing the county and regional population, only selected data were chosen to serve as indicators for identifying conditions that directly cause nonworkers to abstain from pursuing apparent, potential jobs. Variables 13 and 14 were omitted at the first screening because it was believed they would distort the integrity of the "nonworker" definition (see Table 1.6).

A key problem emerged when the county values were aggregated to APDC levels. As in all cases of employing central tendency, the averages developed for the APDCs masked the severity of the extreme low-mobility, low-personal income, and low-labor-force conditions — particularly in the low-density rural counties (see Figure 1.4). Therefore, further analyses were performed at the county level, thus permitting the use of effective sampling techniques for the two counties by employing the speed matrix.

Table 1.6.   Labor Force Unemployed and Median Years of Educational Attainment in Georgia and Its APDCs: 1970–1975

Area	Percent Unemployed, 1975	Median Years Educational Attainment, 1970
United States	8.5%	12.1
Georgia	8.6	10.8
Altamaha Southern	7.2	9.5
Atlanta Metropolitan	9.1	11.9
Central Savannah	8.6	8.7
Chattahoochee Flint	9.4	9.2
Coastal Crescent	7.9	10.1
South Georgia	7.1	9.3
Coosa Valley	9.6	9.2
Georgia Mountains	10.0	9.1
Heart of Georgia	6.4	9.3
Lower Chattahoochee	7.5	8.9
McIntosh Trail	9.1	9.6
Middle Flint	10.2	8.9
Middle Georgia	7.3	10.0
Northeast Georgia	7.6	9.3
North Georgia	10.1	8.6
Oconee Valley	7.1	8.9
Southeast Georgia	8.3	9.1
Southwest Georgia	7.5	9.3

Source: Derived estimates from Georgia Department of Labor, Division of Research and Statistics (1977b) and U.S. Department of Commerce, Bureau of Census (1978a), Table 3, pp. 90–125.

Methodology.   In order to explore mobility/personal income/work activity relationships in rural Georgia, a parametric flow of the circularity was diagrammed for the model as follows:

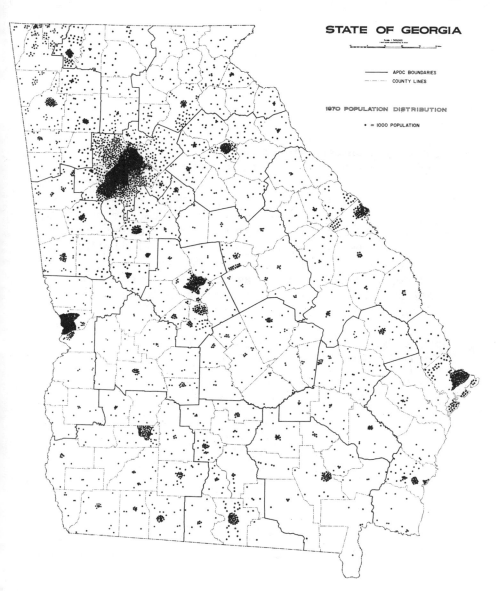

Figure 1.4.   Population Distribution and Density in Georgia: 1970.

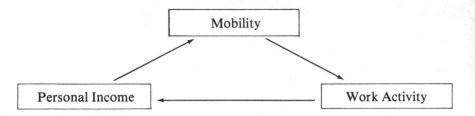

Three key variables are used to measure the relative incidence impinging upon these parameters. Mobility is measured by the incidence of *carless* per geographic area; personal income, by the level of *median income*; and work activity, by the incidence of *labor force participation*. The carless and income variables are applied to households and families, respectively, rather than to individuals. They are assumed to be relatively commensurate; therefore, they have been equated in order to be used interchangeably in this research. Labor force participation is the rate that is derived as a share of the civilian population sixteen years of age and older. The civilian labor force (CLF) is the sum of all gainfully employed inhabitants *plus* the unemployed (individuals *actively* seeking employment), as defined by the U.S. Department of Labor, Bureau of Labor Statistics. The nonemployed segment of the population is the residual between the CLF and the working-age population.

The key measures of the parameters are diagrammed as follows:

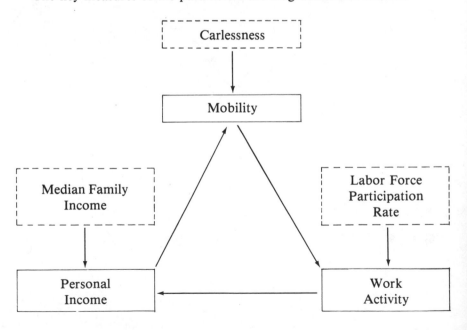

A search of the literature, coupled with discussions with state and local government officials throughout Georgia who are responsible for providing service to the mobility disadvantaged, reveals that no statewide method or procedure exists that will identify a rural transportation clientele. To identify such a clientele requires an information base that describes the characteristics of the mobility disadvantaged. A set of categories was selected for this study from available data sources that generally are used to measure the extent of disadvantages suffered by the target population. The delimitation of rural areas in Georgia was based on the qualitative definition developed by Kaye (1977) for the U.S. Department of Agriculture, Economic Research Service. The Georgia counties were delimited by three designations: urban (U), commuter (C), and noncommuter (N). Their definitions are as follows:

U = an SMSA county or designated urban/county or growth center/ county.

C = a county outer boundary within fifty miles of an urban county/ center.

N = a county outer boundary beyond fifty miles of an urban county/ center.

All other variables were converted from absolute values to relative shares where the shares were indexed against the state share, which, in every case, was normalized to 100. They were then rank-ordered to determine the degree of disadvantage each variable set upon the area.

The following tasks were performed during the analysis through relative share derivations *for all variables that could be quantified* to determine the disadvantages of mobility areally among Georgia's rural inhabitants:

- Incidence of "places" under 5,000 inhabitants;
- Georgia's rural counties;
- Incidence of worker out-county commutation;
- Incidence of carlessness;
- Incidence of labor force participation;
- Levels of personal income;
- Incidence of unpaved county roads;
- Incidence of area poverty;
- Incidence of phonelessness;
- Incidence of area black inhabitants;
- Incidence of area rurality;
- Incidence of area density;

- Incidence of area payments for Aid to Families with Dependent Children.

A factor analysis was performed using the variables listed above. This technique was used to explore relationship patterns among the data presented in this research. The data for the variables at the county level were derived from the sources, noted in the tables above, used to aggregate values to the APDC levels. Factor analysis, as Rummel (1973) posits, will aid in discerning the patterns of profile similarity (Q-mode) of cases and in delineating patterns of variation (R-mode) in characteristics. Each pattern has a different shape, which illustrates what is meant by saying that factor analysis *divides the regularity in the data into its distinct patterns*. In summary, the factor analysis facilitates (1) reduction of voluminous, cumbersome, and complex materials to manageable proportions by isolating a set of meaningful variables and (2) interpretation of the power within a pattern of variables as they relate to each other (North et al., 1963). The definition, description, and rationale for selecting and using these variables are stated in Chapter 4.

Once the relationships among mobility, work activity, and personal income were validated as to their relatively low levels, one rural county was extracted from each of the two geographic areas in Georgia for a more discrete analysis of travel times on selected routes within the county. The results reported in the analysis section reveal some of the constraints that hinder low-income rural inhabitants from getting and keeping jobs that are any significant time or distance from their homes. It also reveals why most of the ongoing and proposed public transportation programs reported in the literature search section cannot service full-time workers who reside in the hinterlands of a given laborshed.

While several programs were examined to determine how the model designed for this research might be applied to Federal Department of Transportation programs, the specific focus is to indicate areas where the most severe devolution for potential workers caused by the deficiencies described by the basic parameters of this research occurs. Furthermore, it permits policy planners to differentiate the work-trip disadvantaged from the nonwork-trip handicapped among the dispersed, isolated, low-income families residing in rural Georgia (Kaye, 1976a). Moreover, it obligates them to attenuate the broad rural transportation issue into categories manageable for those who might rise above the near poverty level if transportation options were available to them. More important, however, the model provides the opportunity to appraise the political constraints that prevail in these jurisdictions, in the responsible agency, and in the legislature.

In the final analysis, the model offers to planners and budgeters a measure of predictive ability heretofore unavailable for their functional process. From this base, policy analysts and management scientists can develop scenarios and strategies through which decisionmakers in the public administration of transportation services can rationally deliberate and select appropriate transit program options for needy people in rural areas.

2 HISTORICAL DEVELOPMENT OF TRANSPORTATION PROBLEMS FOR THE POOR IN RURAL REACHES

The purpose of this chapter is to identify events and trace the changes that have set the stage for the transportation conditions that now exist in rural America. It explores the causes and effects of private sector investment decisions and examines the impact of public investment decisions related to transportation services as they impinge upon the mobility disadvantaged.

To be sure, policy analysis regarding this problem is extremely complex because human demography cannot be regarded as a static feature; instead, as Reynolds (1951) postulates, it oscillates as a dynamic morphology. Haggett has suggested that "physical and social processes leave comparable trails . . ." (in Haggett and Chorley, 1969, p. 32). Furthermore, this dualism between physical and human geography is part of a far wider dualism (Bunge, in Haggett and Chorley, 1969, p. 196). In dealing with work commutation and residential migration from the hinterland, however, it is well to remember that the human condition comprised of experiences and reinforcements prevails. A key element to that condition is *time*. Lear succinctly asserts that it condenses to individual perception as to "how we collect . . ." and value ". . . our minutes" (Kuralt, 1981).

DEFINITION OF TERMS

The following basic definitions are presented as a point of departure for this chapter:

Transportation. Kaye (1976a) defines transportation as the physical means of moving to satisfy the need for mobility.

Mobility. Mobility is the capacity, capability, and opportunity to move. This definition refers to a conveyance such as a four-wheeled vehicle.

Mobility Needs. Mobility needs, defined by Hauser et al. (1975), are systems, services, vehicles, and personnel that are necessary to satisfy total demand requirements.

Mobility Characteristics. Mobility characteristics are data that describe a trip by purpose, distance, origin/destination, frequency, and cost.

The Carless. The carless are defined by Paaswell and Recker (1974) as those households without access to a car (or other vehicle) at the time of need.

Capture Rate. Hauser et al. define capture rate as the proportion of any mobility-disadvantaged group that is expected to use a formal transportation program utilizing vehicles made available from outside the household.

Transit Dependent. The definitions of "transit dependent" and "mobility disadvantaged" differ little. Apparently, the terminology was selected to comport to the themes of the 1968 and 1972 conferences regarding mobility, work activity, and personal income.

John Crain (1972) defines this group as those who are totally dependent on public transportation. The group, identified at the Conference on Transportation and Human Needs (1972), includes those who cannot drive: the young, the poor, the structurally unemployed, the carless members of suburban families, the physically handicapped, and those elderly for whom public transit is totally nonexistent.

Mobility Disadvantaged. Hauser et al. define as mobility disadvantaged any noninstitutionalized, legally and physically licensable person who cannot carry out a reasonable level of desired activity outside the home because of a lack of available vehicle, road facility, or transportation service. Webber (1978) refers to persons who do not have automobiles as "deprived."

Paratransit. "Paratransit," a relatively new concept in the United States, encompasses the many forms of transportation service that fall between the privately owned, self-operated automobile and scheduled, routed transit services. Kirby (1975), of the Urban Institute, notes that paratransit serves as an umbrella for personal transportation service including taxi, jitney, van service, car pools, or any other hired transit. He states that the different types of vehicle involved are not the determinant, but that the type of transportation service offered is the distinguishing characteristic. Paratransit is grouped into three major categories: (1) self-operated rentals, (2) demand-responsive service, and (3) prearranged vehicle pools.

Travel Demand. Travel demand refers to trips *desired* during a period of time by people in a target group or geographic area.

Latent Demand. Latent demand is a component of travel demand that is constrained by factors such as economic condition; it refers to trips that are not made because a constraint cannot be overcome.

Generated Demand. Generated demand is a component of travel demand; it refers to trips actually made (trips generated) by using available systems and resources.

Economically Disadvantaged. The economically disadvantaged are defined in the "1975 Survey of Buying Power" as families whose annual household income falls between the 1974 "effective buying power" level of $8,000 per year and the state median family income level. As Parham (1977) avers, "they are too well off for welfare and too poor to pay" for life support services.

Orshansky (1972) asserts that there is no single, universally accepted and uniformly applicable standard, nor can there be, that can be applied to discern who is poor.

Poverty. Poverty is defined as a condition in which the amount of money available to a family is inadequate to satisfy its needs during a given year. Hence, counts of the poor will be based on a personal, earned, cash-income criterion alone. This criterion allows for establishment of a quantifiable base; but, as Batchelder (1966) discovered, it disregards family size, locational mobility, employment accessibility, and social intercourse.

Rein (1972) posits that the subsistence level definition is arbitrary, circular, and relative; it imposes a number of arbitrary judgments in which the same data can be used to demonstrate that poverty is either a significant or a trivial problem.

Hinterland.   Taafe and Gauthier (1973) suggest that hinterland delimits a spatial zone, or tributary arena, within which the amount of resources expended for a good or service is less than the amount expended for a good or service in an adjacent exchange market or trade area. More specifically, Berry (1967) notes that "hinterland" identifies the "economic reach" from "maximum transit" to an urban center within which a commuter is willing to travel.

Incorporated Places.   Incorporated places include hamlets, villages, towns, and townships that range in size from under 1,000 to 1,000,000 inhabitants or more (Randill, Greenhalfh, and Samson, 1973). These areas include urban systems with 100 inhabitants per square mile (U.S. Department of Commerce, Census of Population, 1970).

Rural Areas.   In developing data summaries, the Census Bureau definition applies the term "rural areas" to all areas outside places of 2,500 persons or more containing under 100 inhabitants per square mile. In the final determination, however, this research considers small towns of up to 5,000 inhabitants as rural in any given application.

Households.   The term "household" is defined as "family" and will be used interchangeably. The definition will conform to that used in the *1970 Census of Population and Housing*.

Network.   A network, defined by Haggett and Chorley (1969), is a meshed fabric of intersecting lines and interstices, *or* a set of geographic locations interconnected in a system by a number of routes. Busaker and Saaty (1965) equate a "graph" to a "network."

TRANSPORTATION/POVERTY LINKAGE: ORIGIN OF RECOGNITION

Toward the end of the 1960s, extensive examination of transportation poverty began to unfold. For example, the American Academy of Arts and Sciences sponsored monthly seminars on the subject. Chaired by Daniel P. Moynihan, the group investigated specific topics related to the urban poverty problem. Among these, it was decided that transportation was of critical importance. The Academy obtained funds from the Departments of Housing and Urban Development and of Transportation to finance a Conference on Transportation and Poverty (1968). John Meyer, president of the National Bureau of Economic Research, organized the project. Meyer, along with John Kain of Harvard University, met regularly with seminar members and representatives of HUD and DOT to explore the relationship of transportation to poverty. The meetings were organized around three topics: (1) jobs and transportation, (2) income redistribution effects, and (3) programs and solutions.

It is apparent that major disparities exist among income classes. An economy with a gross national product of a trillion dollars and employment levels running over 95% of the available work force should have no problem with the distribution of its rewards (Eyestone, 1972). But such is not the case. While a significant drop occurred in the percent of population below the poverty line during the decade of the sixties, according to *Current Population Reports* (U.S. Department of Commerce, 1969), 25.4 million people remained victims of poverty. Based on family size, place of residence, and food costs, the poverty line represents a basic subsistence level more aptly described as a "disenfranchised, diseconomic nightmare" rather than even a modest version of the American Dream. As a result, it does not keep pace with the rise in general living standards. In addition, the poor themselves observe a lifestyle that increasingly diverges from the reality of their lives. They suffer a form of "relative poverty" or "psychological poverty" as a result:

> This kind of poverty is not often recognized because the affluent majority in America sets up a double standard, viewing subsistence as an adequate level for the poor while itself looking to a standard far beyond this basic minimum. [Eyestone, 1972, pp. 149–53]

One curious element about the definition of poverty is that most federal agencies use different criteria in arriving at a so-called poverty line. For example, the Social Security Administration's concept of "near poverty" was $4,700 for an urban family of four in 1969, whereas the "lower living standard" of the Bureau of Labor Statistics was about $6,400 for the same family in that same year. Nevertheless, 44.8 million, or over 23%, of the poor and near poor emphasize that an income floor for subsistence, including effective transportation to jobs, is not at all a radical proposal for the United States. The apparent discrepancy between 25.4 million and 44.8 million stems from the method of counting. The latter quantity includes what Eyestone refers to as "near poor" — those whose personal income falls below the measure of central tendency.

Eyestone distinguishes the poor by categorizing them into four distinguishable classes: aged poor, disabled poor, working poor, and nonworking poor. While substantial overlap inheres in these classes, Falcocchio and

Cantilli's (1974, p. 5) model, "The Universe of Transportation Users," diagrammed in their model, to some degree separates these classes into discrete elements. Their model also identifies the overlaps that occur among the poor, the young, the elderly, and the physically handicapped.

Eyestone's (1972, p. 153) model of the poor defines the causes for each category:

Aged poor: Poor because of inadequate private retirement benefits;

Disabled poor: Poor because of inability to work — or because work is considered unsuitable;

Working poor: Poor because of low skill levels, sporadic job availability, low wages, or large families;

Nonworking poor: Poor because of low skill levels or shortage of jobs; because they are undependable or are labor force dropouts; and other reasons.

To some degree this research addresses Eyestone's "working poor"; in large part it also addresses Ornati's (1969, p. 48) "nonworking poor" who may be undependable solely because of inaccessibility to the job site. It is inconsistent to presume that workers receiving poverty wages can afford to own, operate, maintain, and insure a motor vehicle. As Eyestone asserts, the American Dream has some gaping holes where willing workers are unable to earn enough to support their families even at the poverty line, much less to purchase high-cost transportation of any sort.

Kaye (1976a, pp. 1-5), an expert on the relationship of transportation and the economically disadvantaged, asserts that mobility is essential to conquer poverty. He argues that one of the factors leading to the decline of rural life in America is the lack of mobility. The failure to achieve a more balanced development strategy and the lack of mobility, particularly the lack of reliable, inexpensive human transportation, are beginning to surface as important inhibiting factors to job seeking *and* job keeping. Concomitantly, he notes that rural areas suffer from a disproportionate number of lower-income people. The near poverty group he describes must be included in the number who cannot afford transportation. Experience illustrates that large numbers of this population fall in and out of the poverty group intermittently. He cites several case studies of rural areas where public transit consists of taxicabs only — which are excessively expensive — while other smaller communities do not even offer taxi service.

A U.S. Department of Agriculture (1974) study of labor and social adjustment along the Mississippi Delta in the state of Arkansas found that many respondents expressed dissatisfaction with employment opportunities in the area. Although they did not wish to move elsewhere, they indicated that lack of jobs could force such action. Lack of transportation was a major deterrent to employment. Of those in poverty households, 64% reported they had no means of getting to work, although major industries were located within five to twenty-five miles of their homes.

Such conditions of immobility for the underemployed and rural poor may be the major element that turns otherwise perceived "sweet" industrial development efforts in rural communities sour. The various efforts supported through federal antipoverty legislation over the last fifteen years suggest no cognizance of this accessibility and mobility problem and offer little support for vehicle or facility relief other than reimbursement for travel and/or relocation expenses.

A study by Summers and Lang (1976) suggested that the primary goal and apparent logic behind this industrial relocation strategy are fairly simple. Both rural poverty and urban socioeconomic problems are products of a geographic mismatch of labor supply and demand. One means of correcting this imbalance is to stimulate the rural economy. The study revealed that new factories did not hire the local nonemployed. (Summers and Lang define "nonemployed" to mean the same as Ornati's "nonworker" and Eyestone's "nonworking poor.") In fact, the operations of the local labor market often work against the needs of the people for whom rural industrial development allegedly has been promoted. The people who bear the cost of the development may find themselves in a worse relative position after development than before. The findings suggest that what industry does achieve is a redistribution of the local population rather than movement of people into the area from distant metropolitan areas. Additionally, development has failed to stem the outflow of the young from rural communities. Furthermore, the assumption that industrial development as a technique to promote urban-rural balance was found by the Committee on Agriculture and Forestry (U.S. Congress, 1972a) to be invalid. The committee reported that such may be the case since over half of all the country's counties are significantly removed from jobs and other benefits that generally are available in large cities. The purpose of this study was to identify and describe for the committee the sections of the country that lay beyond the effective commuting field of urban employment centers. However, Walter Wilcox (U.S. Congress, 1972a) of the USDA points out that for policy purposes the conventional rural-urban distinction is of limited value.

During the decade of the sixties, nearly two thousand of the country's most rural counties suffered a 10% net decline in population by outmigration, while nonrural counties gained population through net inmigration. Workers living in rural areas near urban employment centers generally had jobs; less than 10% of the work force in over seventeen hundred of the most rural counties, however, were able to commute into cities for jobs. They had no nearby growth centers on which they could depend. Although these rural counties were less able to provide the facilities and public services required to attract industry, they were already taxing themselves nearly an eighth more heavily in relation to their income than other counties. Yet their local government expenditures for essential activities were only four-fifths as great as those in nonrural counties. Moreover, the incidence of poverty in these most rural of counties was more than double that in the nonrural counties; with 12% of the nation's population, they had 24% of those persons classified as living in poverty.

With high-speed, limited-access freeways, commuting over comparatively long distances is physically possible; indeed, some studies have used criteria of twenty- to fifty-mile radii between home site and employment center to identify large commuting zones around major urban centers. It is significant, however, that the topic of the carless is not mentioned in the USDA study noted above.

The results of urban and rural studies differ strikingly in terms of perspective on distance. Another report for the Department of Transportation (Burkhardt and Eby, 1969) noted that attention now is being given to characteristics other than route structures and distance in journey-to-work patterns in rural areas.

While Wilcox notes that there is a limit to commuter tolerance that contradicts the typical fifty-mile criterion, Falcocchio and Cantilli (1974) found that travel to work by the poor assumes some sort of time-distance constraint. For instance, jobs that are fifteen minutes away are eight times more attractive than jobs located one hour away from the unskilled worker's residence. As travel distance required to reach a job site approaches an hour and a half, the attractiveness of such a job site as a source of employment for a central-city unskilled worker is negligible. Commuting to areas not in the central business district is less convenient — that is, it is more complex, time-consuming, and dearer — for the poor than for the nonpoor (Ornati, 1969).

The inconvenience for commuters is no less a problem in rural than in urban areas. Burkhardt and Eby (1969), in their study of a free-transit demonstration project in West Virginia, found that the average round-trip length of all trips between the rural area and the city of Beckley was forty-five miles. They went on to note that the typical journey-to-work distance in non-SMSA locations substantially exceeded the national average for such trips.

In farm communities, long journey-to-work trips predominate over short ones. Although Summers and Lang's (1976) "Jobs to People" study deals with poverty and economic development rather than transportation, mobility of employees in rural areas from home to workplace is still shown to be extremely important.

The paucity of research in this area is a major problem in attempting to ascertain the variables that affect rural employment commuting patterns. In a study dealing with home-to-work travel, Clemente and Summers note that little is known about work and residence separation in rural areas — largely because urban patterns have been the subject of interest. Further, they found that relationships that had emerged in metropolitan-based research were not paralleled in nonmetropolitan regions. For purposes of my own research, the Clemente and Summers (1975) notion that ecological patterns influence commuting in nonmetropolitan regions supports the assumptions developed previously. In rural areas, unlike large cities, little spatially contiguous housing is available. Rather, small towns and villages serve as housing, but not transit, nodes. Despite the dearth of data, existing evidence suggests that where rural transit is available, revenues and ridership are declining sharply. Simultaneously, as various industrial activities relocate to maximize their return on investment, dependency on the private automobile by the job seeker/holder is increasing. The complexities of dispersion and agglomeration among small communities, whether proximate to or remote from large urban centers, create situations that contradict the underlying concept of public transportation. A case in point is Peachtree Corners, in Gwinnett County (part of the Atlanta SMSA), which contains a huge industrial park adjacent to Atlanta. (Kaye, in his EDA/ERS analysis, defines Gwinnett as a rural county.) The County Commission has chosen not to participate in the Metropolitan Atlanta Rapid Transit Authority (MARTA) and, therefore, work transits from the hinterlands depend almost totally on private automobiles (Clemente and Summers, 1975).

TRANSIT DEPENDENT/MOBILITY DISADVANTAGED

Kaye is one of the few researchers who recognizes that transit dependency is not solely an urban problem. As recently as a decade ago, he began to disaggregate the total population geographically across central-city, suburban, and rural boundaries.

Similarly, Crain (1972), in discussing the problem of "transit-dependent persons," demonstrates in his analysis that rural Americans are equally as transit dependent as urban Americans. Crain asserts, however, that such a disaggregating process is complex because of the great overlap among various transit-dependent categories.

The complexity results from the various criteria assigned to the definition. Crain, like Falcocchio and Cantilli, identifies the poor, the young, the elderly, and the handicapped as transit dependent on some means other than the availability of a privately controlled automobile. Davis and Oen (1977) use two slight variations of the same term — transit dependent — to describe travel immobility. In the introduction to their study, they refer to *transportation-dependent*. In their goal statements they label their target population as "transit dependents."

Surprisingly, Crain found that suburban inhabitants are approximately 20% more transit dependent than central-city dwellers. The extended suburban dependency may result from the paucity of sidewalks in suburbia, which virtually eliminates the "walk mode" that city dwellers enjoy. Paaswell and Recker (1976) note that choice of mode differs when all modes are considered. Obviously, the carless tend to walk more frequently than the noncarless. Those with cars drive, and the next choice is to walk. Moreover, the use of a car as a fare-paying passenger for the noncarless is higher than the use of a bus or taxi. Such "neighboring" is an option, but often a costly one. Even more important for this research, Crain (1972) found that the number of rural poor transit dependents in 1970 exceeded half again the number of central-city poor and almost three times the number of poor in suburbia.

As a strong proponent of rural economic and social development, Kaye (1976a) assigns many of the failures in development to transportation deficiencies that prevail in most rural areas. He declares that a major factor leading to the decline of rural life in America is the lack of mobility, which affects, particularly, a great proportion of southern rural people. Thus he argues that the majority of them are transportation disadvantaged. While addressing households without accessibility either to private automobiles or public transit, he defines rural households without an automobile as "transportation-deprived" households.

Further, Kaye describes rural households with even one automobile as transportation-handicapped households since approximately 87% of rural workers must utilize private automobiles to reach their employment. Kaye defines a group of members in the one-car households as "handicapped" because of their transportation immobility: he refers to nonheads of households who are stranded while the head is at work and the only available household car is parked at the job site.

Kaye developed these definitions to be used by the Economic Development Administration to identify nonurban counties and characteristics of U.S. rural areas with noncommuting populations (USDA, 1972, p. 296), where the incidence of transportation disadvantaged is significant. He labels the counties as "commuter" or "noncommuter" to illustrate the depth of the journey-to-work problem.

It is this "handicapped" label that may generate confusion because of its application to the special needs of the elderly and handicapped population as specified in the original mass transportation act:

> For purposes of this Act, the term "handicapped person" means any individual who, by reason of illness, injury, age, congenital malfunction, or either permanent or temporary incapacity or disability, is unable without special facilities or special planning or design to utilize mass transportation facilities and services as persons who are not so affected. [*U.S. Code:* PL 91–453, 1976]

It is interesting to note that many conditions, while they implicitly suggest physical handicaps, may entail economic incapacity or disability. Kaye explicitly stated that he defined "handicapped" to mean "carless" or "transit dependent" rather than physiologically disabled.

Kaye (1976a) further asserted at the First National Conference on Rural Transportation that policy statements differ from administrative actions. Agriculture Secretary Butz ignored President Ford's promise regarding transportation in early 1976 and shifted the burdens from federal grants to local communities after the president had proposed to include $3.4 billion in his budget for small urban and rural areas through fiscal year 1977 as part of the Unified Transportation Assistance Program (UTAP). The purpose of UTAP funds is to permit states and local communities to determine their transportation priorities for capital improvements, among other needs. UTAP would provide more flexible assistance for public transportation systems in smaller urban and rural areas.

In a society where almost every household apparently owns one or more automobiles, it seems inconceivable, say Meyer and Kain (1968), that a significant number of households are carless. In 1950, six of every ten U.S. households were private car owners; in 1967 these figures had grown to nearly eight of every ten; and by 1972 *more* than eight in ten households were car owners. Thus, 80% of U.S. households own one or more cars. *But* the 20% of U.S. households who do not own cars represent more than 40 million people.

These indicators imply a more complex problem than the mere matter of vehicle ownership. Paaswell and Recker (1974) refer to this factor as the most common denominator to single out specific groups as travel disadvantaged. They posit further that the term *disadvantaged* is used because real penalties are assessed in time, cost, or simply inability to pursue a desired activity when a car is not available. They hasten to note that nonaccess to a car in itself does not represent a homogeneous set of the population. They determine the extent of the problem from household and personal data.

Moreover, more than 65% of the 203 million people residing in the United States in 1970 had no immediate *access* to a car. This number can be enlarged if one includes the physically handicapped and those with cars who choose not to drive because of restricted license or lost insurance. This leads to the following observations:

1. A significant number of people have no car during all or a large part of the day.
2. In a household with one car that is primarily for the work trip by the head of household and that remains at the place of work, the remaining members of the household must respond essentially as members of no-car households during working hours.

While the steady upward progression in automobile ownership has developed for the American population in general, the poor nowhere achieve such a level. In 1968, 47% of family units with before-tax incomes of $2,000 to $2,999 did not own an automobile. Comparative percentages for families in the income ranges of $1,000 to $1,999 and below $1,000 were even higher — 62% and 75%, respectively. The notion, proposed by Meyer and Kain (1968), that the incidence of car ownership increases as income level increases is corroborated by Asin and Svercl (1974). Apparent discrepancies in the frequency of the carless reported in the cited documents stem from different methodologies and sampling techniques employed during their research. About 63% of households with incomes of less than $3,000 annually own a car compared with 99% of households with incomes of $15,000 and over. Since car ownership is related to income, these carless households are probably the poor.

Members of the low-income groups who own automobiles suffer another malady: poor people generally own poor cars. Not only are these cars poor, they are (1) too old and inadequate for long-distance commutation and for expressway operation and (2) usually uninsured.

While for several decades cost figures have been valid for most of the U.S. population, the poor increasingly suffer from extreme regressivity in terms of transport costs. Not only have fuel prices increased significantly, but during the decade between 1967 and 1976, as reported in the *Atlanta Constitution* ("Car Shoppers Kick," 1977), average consumer costs for new cars increased 70%, from $3,200 to $5,450. In one year, from 1975 to 1976, median selling prices increased 14%. While the article did not discuss low-cost models, such price increases can have similar regressive effects on the used-car market where most poor must and do shop. Since the current new-car consumer buys higher-priced, less energy-efficient units, we can forecast a market three to four years hence of used cars that will provide to the poor an energy-inefficient supply of vehicles that their budgets can ill afford.

In rural areas the supply of used vehicles tends to be "more used" than in urban areas where home-to-work distances are significantly smaller. In places of less than 5,000 inhabitants. Svercl and Asin (1973) found that over 45% of the work force travels more than twenty-one miles one way to work, while in places of 100,000 to 1 million inhabitants, less than 24% travels that distance. Thus the rural vehicle travels substantially greater distances between its origins and destinations, obviously costing more money to accomplish the same purpose. With greater use comes more wear. Consequently, maintenance and repairs as well as operation costs are higher for ruralites. Such conditions can impact the poor owner only negatively.

Wheeler (1974), while discussing the paradox of poverty housing in urban areas, counters Owen's argument. He notes that the poor live on the most expensive land in the city in order to obtain low-cost, short-time travel to work. While Wheeler's study deals primarily with urban congestion, the problem in rural sparsity is quite similar but has some differences. In his discussions on the plight of a low-income household, he notes that poor families cannot afford the luxury of high-level mobility. As mentioned in Chapter 1, only those families that are unusually mobile are willing to substitute the inconvenience of long-distance daily commuting for the savings in housing costs associated with the rural environment. But generally, relatively little accessibility to work activity prevails for the poor.

Hunker (1974) addresses this rural transport problem to some degree in his discussion on the relationship between the expanding and changing urban system and rural America, a relationship that is rooted in transportation. While accessibility and mobility have a significant effect on urban living, they also impact heavily the rural areas. Hunker does not overlook the many problems that these effects and other alternatives might impose on small communities. He notes that the report of Nixon's Task Force on Rural Development argues for a more favorable distribution of people on the land in rural areas as opposed to urban concentrations, which would more effectively utilize national resources. Hunker asserts that the report implies that urbanization has failed and that rural America is a suitable replacement. It does not answer, according to Hunker, the perplexing problem of viable alternatives for living and working for rural as well as urban dwellers.

Wheeler, too, notes that directions in travel patterns have reversed since World War II as a result of improved technology: urban-to-rural migration has occurred, with attendant commutation for the journey to work. This reversal has made the longer journey to work even more common. While, as commuters, they live in census-designated rural areas, these people are basically part of the urban population as they work, shop, and visit in the city just like any other urban household. The only real difference, Wheeler posits, is that these folk prefer a rural residence. He refers to them as the frontiersmen of the urban domain. Further, he notes that the rural resident, forced out of agriculture by declining profits, has two choices: either to migrate to the city or to commute to urban employment.

Compounding the problem for both poor urban denizens and poor rural migrants renting from absentee owners is the "regentrification" movement occurring from neighborhood revitalization in older areas (Peirce, 1979). Displacement of the diseconomic and disenfranchised is justified by Seegrist (1981) on the basis of reestablishing the "old" culture of yesteryear. More than likely, it is sheer economic exploitation of the poor by the "unseen hand" of the marketplace. To be sure, it is an elitist point of view that deserves serious examination by policy analysts and decisionmakers before wholesale "revitalization" efforts destroy the subculture of the "unwashed." The key question concerning this recent trend is, Where do these denizens find adequate living quarters following their eviction? Next, What effect does such a move have on the displaced, victimized tenant's job situation? Ultimately, Does the displacement hamper work commuting for the displaced poor? Finally, Are the neighborhoods really revitalized, or do we have enclaves of suburbanites who have clasped onto the fashionable trend in nouveau urban living? On the other hand, to restrict regentrification by enactment, mandate, or coalition flies in the face of private enterprise and personal proprietorship.

Hunker states that rural dwellers are often willing to commute long distances to manufacturing sites to obtain a relatively high industrial wage while retaining the qualities of rural lifestyle they find desirable. In many southern states and mountain areas, the labor pool often covers a relatively extensive geographic region around a key employment center. Those who opt for labor force exit equate to Ornati's "nonworkers" — that is, those who suffer the problem of "structural" or chronic unemployment as defined by Kohler (1968). The Clark subcommittee refers to members of this group as the "involuntarily unemployed" who no longer actively seek work. This inaction further exacerbates the problem of labor choices among the ghetto poor (Falcocchio and Cantilli, 1974).

Ferman (1969) states that his package for job development in rural areas may include development of a transportation system to ensure geographical mobility from workers' residences to places of employment. Further, Ferman proposes several alternative solutions for providing spatial mobility to potential workers in depressed rural areas. But he notes that his proposed solutions are not always possible. First, he submits that cars, which the poor often do not own, are needed. Also, cost-cutting car pools are required, or rescheduled bus routes are mandated. Second, he suggests boarding workers, weekly, near employment, with arranged weekend commuting. Third, Ferman posits that subsidized relocation of workers and their families might be a viable alternative. The latter two, while solving an economic problem, often carry social problems with them as well. Many low-income families are reluctant to pluck their roots from family surroundings to venture into uncertainties of unknown new areas.

As reported above, some of Ferman's proposals were written into the economic development legislation of the 1960s. In most cases, the early acts did not provide even for transportation costs. In preparing subsequent legislation, it became apparent to the designers of the bills that although training programs were formulated and operating, many members of the target groups were unable to avail themselves of these opportunities because they had no money or vehicles to participate in the manpower development program. The later bills and amendments included provisos for monies to fund transit or relocation. In either case, the legislation assumed availability of privately owned automobiles or some operating transit system by which the trainee could commute or migrate "door through door" to the program locations. Ferman recognizes the problems of the proposed migration alternatives and suggests relevant cautions. Saltzman (1975) refers to this concept for special groups suffering from immobility (physically handicapped) as an adjunct to "door-to-door" service for work trips.

Ferman (1969) states that the migration solution, while quite rational in labor market theory, offers some dangers. Relocation of hard-to-place workers to new communities should be planned carefully. Further, it involves more than furnishing a bus ticket.

Although Ferman does recognize the mobility problem and its attendant social problems, he apparently does not recognize fully the problem of mobility from home to work activity sites. His proposal for a five-member manpower development team includes: (a) a job market analyst, (b) an employment specialist, (c) a placement specialist, (d) a job development specialist, and (e) a job coach. Nowhere in his schemata for the role structure of the job development team does he prescribe a transportation specialist.

Ferman's works should not be maligned too harshly, however, As we have noted, the linkage between transportation and poverty traditionally has not been understood. Other experts working in manpower development and in public transportation began only in the late sixties to explore the problem of linking poverty and employment with the lack of transportation. Prior to the decade of the sixties, no mention was made in either the literature or legislation about mobility or accessibility. And it was not until Section 147 of the 1973 Highway Act was passed to enable rural demonstration programs for public transportation that the problem of job accessibility affecting rural inhabitants was addressed by transportation policy formulators.

The legislation dealing with the "poor," "persistent underemployment," and "public transportation" is discussed more fully in Chapter 3. The housing acts between 1937 and 1959 (*U.S. Code:* PL 86–372, 1960) make no mention of the poor or of transportation. The 1961 Area Redevelopment Act (*U.S. Code:* PL 87–27, 1962) does not include transportation issues, and the 1962 Manpower Development Training Act (*U.S. Code:* PL 88–214, 1963) provides for relocation costs only if the participant moves, which is a significant misperception of the problem.

Accessibility: A Case Study Analysis

In reference to accessibility, it is striking that lack of transportation for the poor was not considered a major factor in joblessness. It is even more striking that the seeming "indifference" by the poor toward seeking work was not recognized by manpower authorities and labor experts as perhaps not indifference at all, but rather resignation to an unsatisfactory and cumbersome transportation arrangement. Needless to mention, jobs located beyond the termini of buslines often go begging because members of the carless nonemployed cannot reach them.

Construction work, for example, does not remain in a single location for a substantial period. Even for huge projects that last two or three years, transit companies do not adjust their itineraries to accommodate the transit dependent among the construction gangs. For, as Liebow (1967) notes, construction employment has its own objective set of disadvantages. It is seasonal work for most workers and operates primarily as a function of dry weather, with irregularity in the cold, wet seasons. Muddy conditions last for long periods. The weather conditions for this type of activity wreak havoc on conventional transit systems if the construction activity is the basis upon which the transit service operates. Moreover, Liebow asserts that the elements are not the only hazard. As the project moves from one construction stage to another, laborers are laid off — usually without warning — sometimes for weeks at a time, or sometimes permanently. The more fortunate or the better workers are told periodically to withdraw from work for two or three days. It is evident that if public transit is nonexistent, the "more fortunate" must possess or obtain an alternative transport system if they are to maintain continual work. It is obvious that a system that charges a nominal fare cannot endure for long without subsidy if demand is as erratic as indicated by the situation described above. The alternatives are private ownership or car pooling with co-workers who live in the neighborhood or who happen to travel a route nearby. This kind of match, however, is not always easy.

Segregation: A Special Social Problem

Meyer and Kain (1968) discuss the special problem caused by racial segregation. They note that housing segregation robs the low-income black of many adjustments that are available to low-income whites. If the job of a low-income white worker shifts to the suburbs, he usually is able to follow it. Frequently, he will be able to relocate his residence to be near a transit line serving his workplace. The low-income black worker is seldom so fortunate, however. Regardless of his income or family situation, he will find it almost impossible to move from the ghetto or from farm areas. If his job moves to the suburbs, it is unlikely he will be able to follow it. Likewise, if a job occurs in a small town, he will be unable to pursue it. Thus for him the service characteristics, coverage, and cost of the transportation system are especially critical. Even if his outlying workplace is served by a transit system, as some are beginning to be, he often will be unable to move to an area served by that particular transit line. If the black is able to reach a suburban workplace at all by public transit, the trip will usually be expensive, circuitous, and multimodal and will require numerous time-consuming transfers. A job must be particularly desirable for anyone, including the low-income black worker, to make the expensive, time-consuming trip by transit or to pay the additional cost of automobile transportation. If he is particularly lucky, he may be able to car pool with a fellow worker and share the often considerable expense of a long-distance trip from remote areas. In some instances, his income will be no lower if he refuses the job and remains unemployed.

Automobile Ownership: The Georgia Condition

A more definitive indicator of transportation is reported in a U.S. Department of Transportation state-of-the-art document (1976c). For purposes of the document, nonmetropolitan places indicate rural areas since both denote low-density population areas. The department reports that over 83%

of the households in nonmetropolitan areas own at least one automobile compared to 77% in metropolitan areas. It is striking that in Georgia the seven-county Atlanta region, the major metropolitan area of the Southeast, does not follow that pattern. In 1970, only 6% of the households in the Atlanta region were carless (see Table 1.2). On the other hand, according to the 1970 *Census of Housing*, two of the three regions in Georgia in which the carless exceed 20% — Oconee with 21% of its households, and Middle Flint with 23% of its households — are highly rural (59% and 63%, respectively). The third region, Lower Chattahoochee, with 26% of its households carless, is only 19% rural. To some degree, the Lower Chattahoochee region's deviation can be explained by the relatively high incidence of military families whose heads of households are stationed at Fort Benning.

These indicators do not depict fully the entire situation, however. In the Lower Chattahoochee eight-county region, three counties are 100% rural, two are more than 90% rural, and one is more than 50% rural. The remaining two counties contain 83% of the region's 232,000 inhabitants. The other approximately 40,000 people reside on 82% of the land, with a density of less than 19 people per square mile, as compared to almost 79 inhabitants for the state — a sparsely populated area indeed.

Road Network

Several designated federal and state highways, as part of the total network, transverse the Lower Chattahoochee region, but they are only a small portion of the total roadway system. In nonurban areas the county road system is greater in terms of miles than the statewide system by a ratio of four to one. County roads and local city streets are constructed with and maintained by county and municipal revenues usually funded by the general fund. Some of these projects are funded by HUD and HEW programs as well as DOT county contract projects. Various combinations of funding sources are employed by county commissioners to finance road and street construction. These roads and streets, according to Lamb (1975-1979), do not include the numbered routes within the city or town limits. These numbered routes remain the responsibility of the state.

The statewide network consists of all state and federal highways, as well as the interstate system, and comprises the entire numbered route system including those within the local areas. Interurban buses operate only along these numbered highways. The governor's office Executive Summary (Georgia, 1974) states that this bus service represents one of the most underutilized of transportation resources. Reportedly, this bus service is relatively inexpensive and can be flexible to satisfy demand without the burdensome capital cost required by fixed rail. Unfortunately, however, the majority of potential users do not live on or near these numbered highways nor do they use fixed rail, since passenger lines are almost nonexistent. The excess capacity exists on line-haul routes with large buses. While the structure of costs in this industry is similar to that of trucking, there is a relatively constant line-haul cost for various lengths of the trip. Furthermore, according to Meyer et al. (1960), the average load increases with the length of haul. As a result of this variation in average load, as well as the need to spread attendant costs over a larger number of units, the passenger-mile costs for trips under fifty miles are approximately 50% greater than for trips over 200 miles. Even if both the origin and destination for rural workers were on the main line, passenger-mile costs over short distances would make daily work travel very expensive.

Meyer et al. state that fully distributed bus costs are low with relatively high load factors. Actual occupancy rates, though, are only about 27%, so the fully distributed passenger-mile cost is inadequate to cover costs. Since bus-operating revenues (excluding special charter services) are so low, this creates a "bus-passenger deficit" problem analogous to the better-known "rail-passenger deficit." But this low load factor with its attendant deficit is largely a consequence of the highly traveled routes between small towns. For operations connecting the major cities, the load factor is probably nearer 75%, and the cost per passenger mile is about half the cost to consumers residing in small towns.

The Movement of Passengers

Meyer et al. note that intercity bus operations are carried on by a relatively large number of firms, and most operate on small local routes. The industry is dominated by Greyhound. On one hand, the intercity bus represents reasonably low-cost transportation. Its flexibility and small unit of operation give it a place in public transportation markets between smaller cities and on short hauls. But a trend that began in the late forties continues: the passenger car is both the most popular and generally the cheapest means of passenger transport in North America. Little competition from other firms in the industry prevails; that which does exacerbates an unprofitable situation for the operators. The profitable runs that do exist are the long line hauls, as mentioned above, which do not fit the rural model. Line hauls are nonstop runs between two high-density stations. These hauls assume a high load factor, which usually generates substantial profits. Because of price and route regulation by the Interstate Commerce Commission, the industry's viability has suffered for about a quarter-century. Despite such regulation and the absence of competition, the entire industry has become unprofitable in recent years.

Select companies such as Greyhound and Continental Trailways, the nation's leading long-distance passenger carriers, have been profitable, while smaller companies have encumbered large deficits. The continued successes of Greyhound and Trailways derive from profits generated on high-volume runs. These profits have helped defray deficits on requested low-volume runs that they are not permitted to abandon. Another source of revenue that these two carriers share is their package and freight service. Smaller carriers, according to the Georgia Public Service Commission, are not equipped with compatible vehicles or termini to provide such service.

Aggregate route service has barely covered expenses. Consequently, profits generated by the bus industry are derived largely from reliance on charter service and other operations.

The problem of regular route deficits is particularly acute for the small firms that have less opportunity for auxiliary enterprises. Traffic originating in small towns generally has extremely low average load levels. This may result from an insistence by state commissions on too frequent service to and from small towns. Since both short hauls and low-density routes are concentrated among the small carriers, these two factors intensify the problems of the small firm in the bus industry.

The purpose of these discussions on public transportation conditions prevailing two decades ago is to point out that the problem has festered for a long time. Equally important is the fact that line hauls, albeit on the short-distance runs, have experienced problems too, although the industry is carefully protected by iron-clad regulation. The ultimate result of these unprofitable conditions, reported by Bush (1977–1978), has been a rash of applications for decertification and abandonment, even along the formerly profitable runs.

Ironically, it was learned from the World Bank (Millard, 1981) that this issue in the United States is more complex than in Third World countries; thus it is more difficult to solve here. High employment costs in this labor-intensive industry render alternative solutions nearly impossible. Either of the two most common scenarios is attacked with equanimity. First, states Gilstrap (1981), taxes based on service provided, such as zone fares based on passenger mileage carried, are resisted strongly by users even in affluent suburban areas. Assuredly, such pricing is prohibitive in hinterlands, particularly on byways in remote counties. Second, counters Stockman (1981), services and facilities subsidized from the public treasury fall under constant scrutiny, if not severe criticism, when financed federally. Current policy mandates that state or local governments will finance their own. In either case, a tremendous social and/or economic cost inheres in the regulated public transit phenomenon.

On the other hand, free exchange in the private enterprise marketplace can be as devastating, notes Millard (1981). Most developing countries within the purview of the World Bank hold no restriction upon entry into rural jitney service. Subsequently, supply exceeds demand in rural areas encumbering large proportions of the market's fare box revenues such that operators cannot afford maintenance and repairs. Thus the machines fail or become unkempt and unsafe — ultimately resulting in bankruptcy. As of this writing the Transportation, Water, and Telecommunications Department of the World Bank is preparing a position paper on the pitfalls of an unprotected transit industry.

Georgia also has its problems. Although no mention of rural transit problems is made throughout the Georgia (1974) *Executive Summary*, that report does assert a decline in bus service, which indicates problems for some Georgia localities situated some distance from the freeways. Although there is currently adequate transportation among urban areas along the interstate highways, the trend toward eliminating stops between urban areas deprives smaller communities of service. It becomes apparent that if towns along the interstates are being bypassed, the short hauls in and out of rural communities will be lessened if not eliminated. It is safe to conclude, then, that if the small communities lose their accessibility, the surrounding hinterlands that are linked by the county road system — assuming service was provided — probably will be abandoned totally by the carriers.

It is not just the interurban traveler who is of concern to state policy planners. Nor is it the chronic public assistance recipient, handicapped or elderly. Rather, it is the low-income wage earner who is so severely impacted by rising transportation costs that he or she either seeks other employment or withdraws from the labor force. It is the commuter who lives along these rural roads, both county and state, and travels distances of approximately fifty to sixty miles to the workplace. It is the low-income commuter who lives along the state and county roads and who does not own a private automobile. In the final analysis, reiterates Garrity of the governor's office, all the conditions described above condense into inaccessibility to places of employment for a moderate salary in a reasonable length of time, without inconvenience and indignity, but with the safety, regularity, and security afforded the affluent and the mobile urbanite.

The condition of the county road system exacerbates Georgia's problems. These rural roads — with dipping turtlebacks, hazardous hairpin curves, and steep dropoffs — are built along old draft animal paths and are barely wide enough to allow oncoming vehicles to pass. Often roadways were not built to set standards commensurate with the terrain contours or soil load-bearing qualities. With the exception of those roads located in close proximity to densely populated regions or in urban areas, many roads are not even paved. Any hard-surfaced improvements, using a sort of aggregate and bituminous mix, extend only to the traveled edge — without berms. Their thin layers require inordinate amounts of pothole patching with "hotmix" — a quick and easy method for repairing dangerous ruptures at minimal cost. These ruptures occur because the surfacing conforms only to minimum standards. It is along these roads that a substantial proportion of Georgia's rural poor reside.

Until recently Georgia's country highways were in the best physical condition in their history; but the county roads have not been given the attention accorded state and urban roads. Rural county improvement programs have lagged significantly behind other state systems. Subsequently, the condition of the rural county network is not adequate to withstand the pounding of heavy bus traffic or frequent start and stop traffic. These physical factors constrain the operation of conventional public conveyances.

Batchelder asserts that such problems result in inadequate or no local transportation systems. Because of the poverty in such areas, many residents do not own automobiles. Public transportation is not a profitable enterprise because of the low density of development, the great dispersion of dwelling units, and the relatively low travel demand. Travel by foot and by vehicles owned by friends and relatives characterizes the majority of trips. These conditions severely limit the total number of trips by the poor (Batchelder, 1966).

Burkhardt and Eby note another significant problem related to physical transportation facilities. The usability of the rural transportation network is constrained under conditions of inclement weather. In some rural areas, all-weather roads are nonexistent (see Table 1.3). Thus persons in these areas are isolated for a substantial portion of the year. Extensive all-weather road systems may not be justifiable because of the low potential volume of traffic in such sparsely developed areas. The existing transportation system, therefore, may have to be augmented by some sort of emergency service (Burkhardt and Eby, 1969). It can be argued that although emergency service should be provided, a more permanent system is needed to alleviate the underemployment of poor residents in rural areas. This is true in rural Georgia.

Although this research is not designed to survey the inhabitants, the community leaders, or the county commissioners, conversations with various officials in the Area Planning and Development Commissions confirm the need for public transportation to serve a clientele that requires journey-to-work service.

Representing the Planning and Programming Director of the Georgia Transportation Department, I made field visitations to meet with officials of the Area Planning and Development Commissions. These meetings were designed to elicit comments and opinions that would assist the Policy Planning Office in analyzing the extent of need for public transportation in rural Georgia. All eighteen districts were visited in late 1976. A memorandum report and sketch plan entitled "Critical Needs in Georgia's Statewide Transportation System" was submitted to Director Florence L. Breen, Jr. (December 10, 1976). It summarized needs for the handicapped and elderly. Problems concerning the poor and the young, although defined in the original scope of the report, were not explored in the final analysis.

The condition of Georgia's poor is not unique; poverty in rural areas pervades the entire country. But it is particularly pervasive in the Southeast region of the United States. While the condition of Georgia cannot be generalized to every case in the United States, the findings and recommendations, in some measure, can be applied to other states with similar problems.

Low Densities

A pattern of rural-to-urban migration significantly influences the demographic/socioeconomic complex in the rural areas of America. Causes for the migration are many. Labor-intensive, self-sustaining farming historically was the major economic activity in these areas. Significant changes resulting from technological advances have severely altered the industrial mix and, subsequently, the occupational requirements in rural laborsheds.

Voluminous information has been written on this topic in economics, sociology, geography, and political science texts; in monographs; and in journals. Farm youth who seek jobs that do not exist migrate to urban areas for jobs, leaving a skeleton population behind. The skeleton population faces the worst elements of socioeconomic indicators that describe a poor quality of life. These include sparse density, low income, low labor force participation, low educational attainment, high rates of dilapidated housing, and high proportions of youth and elderly. Relatively high rates of nonwhite inhabitants experiencing significantly lower rates of educational attainment than their white counterparts suffer disproportionately because of few or no job opportunities.

Burkhardt clearly states that inadequate transportation has particularly serious impacts on the lives and welfare of the rural poor. Transportation may be a severe problem for the urban poor, but they can still walk or use mass transit to reach a wide range of activities, long-distance trips notwithstanding. This is not true of the rural poor, posits Gurin (1976). Distances are great, and terrain and weather may be forbidding. Consequently, available modes of purchasable transportation are expensive. Moreover, the very isolation of the rural poor can deprive them of awareness of the society and polity around them and, hence, of their own situation and its potential remedies suggests Burkhardt (1969). Part of this situation is their economic condition; part is their social condition. The economic condition is tied to their transit dependency. Without access, they are immobile.

Butts (1972), summarizing the various needs of transit dependents in rural areas, affirms that for many, such as those transit dependents who could attend vocational/technical school or other education training programs, transportation is the key to economic advancement and security. After gaining employment, these individuals, among others who are already working, must have a way to and from their jobs. In cases where transportation is not available, attendance declines and turnover in jobs and training programs increases severely because people lack dependable means of travel.

Batchelder (1966) discusses some federal government ARA/EDA programs that foster the relocation of job seekers by helping to finance the geographic movement of workers and businesses. The federal government has used grants and loans experimentally to help workers move from areas of job scarcity to areas of labor shortage in private employment. While such programs may solve some immediate economic problems for the employer and employee, Batchelder suggests they may concurrently cause more social problems for people who typically would prefer not to move.

Batchelder points to significant conditions relating to free choice — including "grass-roots" familiarity with their home-place, exceptionally strong family ties, and fear of the unknown urban environment — about which the framers of legislation to alleviate poverty apparently were imperceptive and insensitive. The rural poor prefer to stay within at least weekly — if not daily — commuting distance of their native surroundings. Even though the dollars remaining from an urban paycheck after paying for urban rent and food may well be above available rural earnings, many of these people prefer to stay in their rural homes. Perhaps jobs and other special services should be brought to those who choose to remain.

In referring to the riots in Watts in Los Angeles, Batchelder notes that the Watts situation appeared to typify a developing big-city pattern in which public transportation was arranged to connect the middle-class suburbs with the central-city mercantile and industrial centers while leaving the inner-city low-income areas without means of transportation, except for private automobiles or feet. Like Liebow, he asserts:

> It is not enough for a man to be able to do a job, nor is it enough for him to know of a job that he can do — he must be able to *get* to the job. [Batchelder, 1966, p. 181]

In the same vein, Ornati (1969, pp. 12–14) states that accessibility to work from home is more than simply traveling from an origin to a destination. Relative convenience determined by time, cost, and complexity impinge upon the decision to travel, as does the existence of transit itself. In this regard, Ornati (1969, p. 50) found that in urban areas accessibility is constrained more by unfamiliarity than by lack of service. Getting lost is easy.

Social Factors

From a social standpoint, it is believed that educational attainment variables are among the factors that shape the profile of the rural poor. Nobel (1972) believes that in many rural counties in this country illiteracy approaches 25 percent of the adult population because of inadequate transportation to schools.

One may argue that in rural Georgia all school-age children have access to school transportation. Closer scrutiny, however, may indicate that accessibility does play a role. If the transit service — school bus or alternative — is poor, professes Gess (1973–1978), it may encourage eligibly aged students to drop out from society and the economy as well as from school.

Although difficult to corroborate without supporting evidence of an attitudinal survey, low educational attainment rates do suggest that students from poor families drop out of school because attendance is fruitless. It is reasonable to believe that their schooling leads to no job market because no jobs exist in the immediate area; where jobs do exist, there is no way to get to them even if high-cost transportation passed within moderate proximity to their homes (see Table 2.1).

In this context, Nobel states emphatically:

> Transportation for rural people is an issue of survival, not convenience. . . . The rural people have three choices at present: move to the city, go on welfare, or die. [Nobel, 1972, p. 182]

The 1972 USDA study focuses on rural employment commuter patterns and their relationship to county socioeconomic characteristics. It reinforces

Table 2.1   Labor Force Participation, Percent Unemployed, and Median Years of Educational Attainment for Selected Counties in Rural Georgia: 1970–1976.

Area	Labor Force Participation Rate, 1975	Percent Unemployed, 1976	Median Years Educational Attainment, 1970
United States	61.8%	8.5%	12.1
Georgia	61.5	8.6	10.8
Dawson County	50.0	19.3	8.4
Baker County	51.1	7.3	8.5

Source: Derived estimates from Georgia Department of Labor, Division of Research and Statistics (1977b, Table 6, p. 191) and U.S. Department of Commerce, Bureau of Census (1978a, Table 3, pp. 90–125).

Nobel's assertions. Some of the findings in the USDA Economic Research Service report are quite revealing about the economic constraints on the poor in rural areas.

ADDITIONAL TRANSPORTATION COMPLEXITIES

The complexities of transportation and the economy are not new (Maggied, 1967a). Human inability to negotiate changes in personal economy dates back to the Biblical classic of Cain and Abel in Genesis. The saga is symbolic of humanity's inability to change lifestyle from a transitionary pastoral existence to a stationary agricultural economy. A similar problem has pervaded to the present day, when the economy has evolved from the rural agricultural era through the urban manufacturing era during the first half of the present century to the current highly technologized society and polity. Each of these economic scenarios evolved from a relationship of subsistence farming, fishing, and herding to high-speed transportation and mobility.

Part of that mobility acts on human economy and accessibility to employment; that is, employment participation rests on the ability to move from home to work and back, whether in an urban type of materials processing operation, a support service activity, or an extractive industry — agriculture, silviculture, mining — in remote rural reaches. Wherever these activities locate, some form of transportation is required to facilitate these transits, since most human movement in any region throughout rural America is associated with transits for employment (Maggied, 1967b).

Similarly, the work transits in rural Georgia command an efficient *and* economically feasible transportation system for effective people movement, as well as cargo shipments, between residences and job stations regardless of community size or spatial configuration. This is no simple task when all the complexities associated with transportation systems are considered. Such a proviso is a substantial order; transportation is complex because of its dynamic interrelationship between the object of movement and the vehicle to carry it over the facility that connects two or more points in a space module.

The case of rural Georgia has its unique geographic, demographic, economic, political, social, and legal considerations that are consequences of federal and state legislation, regulation, policy, and programs. These considerations differ from those of other states and regions and must be investigated separately to determine their impact on the changes in society, the economy, and the mobility of the rural poor. As Peter Goldmark postulates with respect to the New Rural Society:

> Rural areas in the U.S. differ with regard to the conditions which lead to social and economic inadequacies, although the outcomes of such inadequacies may appear similar. No single study can be generalized to all rural areas. [Goldmark, 1976, p. iv]

It is necessary, therefore, to understand how the conditions evolved that produced the economic and social imbalance between rural and urban Georgia. Moreover, to gain that understanding requires an exploration of the events over time emanating from federal and state enactments, organizations, and programs that dealt with rural housing, transportation, and other infrastructural elements that impact rural Georgians. Additionally, neither transportation, nor communications, nor electrification, nor housing, nor sewage disposal, nor water distribution alone offers a singular solution to community development.

While the economic problem for the poor in rural areas resembles that of the urban poor, national political institutions have not treated different-sized communities of the poor evenhandedly. Insensitivity to rural problems is demonstrated by the dual standards applied to rural issues by the designers of federal legislation.

Events have occurred that relate directly to Georgia's rural transportation condition. To appreciate fully the impacts of these events, it was necessary to review the legal and administrative actions. While the process of uncovering these events was pervasive and complex, it was felt that this search and the synopsis of the lengthy findings were sorely needed to provide a solid grounding for this investigation regarding the dynamics of transportation for work commuters in rural America.

A trace through the history of legislation, programs, and projects pertaining to communities and transportation illustrated the vast difference in provisions between urban and rural legislative entitlements. In the next chapter, some of the highlights of enactments designed to alleviate poverty but that omitted the rural poor are discussed.

3 RURAL LEGISLATION OR RUBRICAL LEGERDEMAIN

Prior to the Rural Development Act of 1972, enactments by Congress did not focus specifically on the issue of poverty in rural areas. More particularly, none dealt with the problems of spatial mobility, job accessibility, and temporal distance of the rural economically disadvantaged. Each can be analyzed statically, but doing so obviates the relationships between the problems. Isard (1975) uses his "crude" gravity model to define commuting fields in any type of communication or transportation phenomenon. This model captures a number of distance-related barriers to interchange besides the purely physical one; these include social distance, psychological (temporal) distance, political distance, and economic (transportation-cost) distance. Legislation dealing with unemployment, economic development, and substandard housing of the poor was aimed almost entirely at urban areas (*U.S. Code:* PL 86-372, 1960; PL 87-70, 1962). The legislation did not address the absence of gravitational "pulls" inherent in rural demographic sparsity (Isard, 1975).

Now, after only two decades of some rural focus and a single decade of programs dealing with rural mobility, the new administration proposes to dismantle the legislative and organizational underpinnings of programs designed to reduce poverty in the nation's hinterlands. Newly elected President Ronald Reagan, in his 1981 "Economic Message" to Congress in joint session, proposed elimination of the Economic Development Administration, which has been a major mechanism for rural infrastructural innovation.

Annotations of and commentary on legislation designed to alleviate rural poverty, immobility, and nonwork are documented below.

THE LEGISLATION

Area Redevelopment Act of 1961

The Area Redevelopment Act of 1961 was one of the first in a series of such acts during the "New Frontier" Kennedy Administration. The House Committee on Banking and Currency, in Section 2 of its Declaration of Purpose, stated that the federal government, in cooperation with the states, would help areas to take effective steps in planning and financing the economic redevelopment of communities, industries, enterprises, and individuals through the establishment of stable and diversified local economies and improved living conditions. Under the provisions of this act, new employment opportunities would be created by developing and expanding indigenous resources rather than by merely transferring jobs from one area to another (*U.S. Code:* PL 87–27, Vol. 1, 1962).

In formulating standards for these areas of persistent underemployment, the legislation mandates that the proportion of low-income farm families as a share of total farm families be identified to ascertain (a) the availability of manpower in each rural area for supplemental employment, (b) the extent of each area's outmigration, and (c) the proportion of population that receives public assistance from either the federal or the state government. The exact definition of "availability of manpower" is not clear, but it presumably refers to the jobless at their place of residence, measured by some statistic (*U.S. Code:* PL 87–27, Vol. 2, 1962).

No mention of transportation is made, except under the "Occupational Training" section. While most of the provisions in Section (d) relate to urban areas, Section (f) enables the administration to give special consideration to the need of agricultural workers; however, that need is not specified (*U.S. Code:* PL 87–27, Vol. 1, 1962).

Manpower Redevelopment Act of 1962

Under Title II, "Training and Skill Development Programs," a provision is made for various weekly training allowances for a period of one year (*U.S.*

Code: PL 87–415, Vol. 1, 1962). The legislation authorizes payment by the Department of Labor of sums necessary to defray transportation and subsistence expenses when training facilities are not within commuting distance of the trainee's regular place of residence. Section 208 of this act provides for pilot projects to relocate unemployed workers to areas where jobs for which they are qualified are available. This demonstration program is designed to increase labor mobility among the retrained unemployed. The initial concern was that transportation costs constrained migration to viable labor market areas. Grants authorized to assist the qualified job seeker could not exceed 50% of the expenses required to move his family (*U.S. Code:* PL 88–214, Vol. 1, 1963).

Housing Act of 1964

Title V addresses the problem of rural housing. Section 516 authorizes financial assistance provisions for public agencies or private nonprofit organizations to engage in programs for low-rent housing and related facilities. The target population of this program is domestic farm labor. The rents charged cannot exceed the income and earning capacity of the tenants, and the housing must be suitable for dwelling use by domestic farm labor (*U.S. Code:* PL 88–560, Vol. 1, 1965). Later acts permit rural residents to finance housing units, including mobile homes (*U.S. Code:* PL 89–754, Vol. 3, 1967; 90–448, Vol. 2, 1969; 93–382, Vol. 1, 1975).

Urban Mass Transportation Act of 1964

The focus of the Urban Mass Transportation Act is urban; the emphasis of the capital improvements is on centroids such as fixed-rail systems directed toward central business districts with a rigidly scheduled feeder-bus subsystem that services exurbia. Typically, population growth to a level of 1 million inhabitants in an urbanized area, as experienced by Atlanta, Georgia, in the sixties, signifies a "need" for a fixed-rail system. Such a system is intended to reverse the overwhelming trend away from public transit commutation by the growing number of automobile owners. However, this legislation gives no consideration to the need for operating subsidies to the transit ownership (*U.S. Code:* PL 88–365, Vol. 2, 1965).

This act was aimed at approximately a dozen cities whose populations exceeded 1 million. It was concerned primarily with extensions of existing "trunk-line" systems that exacerbated current transportation problems of station parking, split modes, and ghetto isolation, among other attendant drawbacks. Among its salient features is enabling legislation to broaden the parameters of an urban issue (which previously had been treated in a fragmented, case-by-case manner) to a national level. The most important factor in this transportation legislation is the shift of emphasis from commodity movement to people transit, albeit to convenience suburban commuters in their journey to work. Nevertheless, this law set the stage for identifying and tying together several transportation, economic, and social problems in both urban and rural areas that heretofore had been ignored or undefined. Rural transportation problems, however, are not specifically mentioned.

Economic Opportunity Act of 1964

This act was designed as major policy to eliminate the paradox of poverty by providing everyone in the country the opportunity for education and training, to work and to live in dignity and decency (*U.S. Code:* PL 88–452, Vol. 1, 1965).

Among the many programs to evolve from this legislation was one to help destitute rural families to increase their income through small capital grants. Another encouraged states to use public assistance as an instrument for helping families lift themselves out of poverty (*U.S. Code:* PL 88–452, Vol. 2, 1965). Under Part A of Title II, communities were offered ample flexibility in providing financial assistance for action programs designed and conducted at a community level — provided that the programs confronted basic problems and held out real promise for their elimination.

Title III proposed to meet some special problems of rural poverty. This part authorized uniquely designed programs to bring practical, income-creating assistance to poor farmers for the first time. Section 302 authorized one-time grants of $1,500 per family to alleviate nonagricultural real estate problems. The section also authorized the financing of $2,500 for enterprises that would supplement farm income. Furthermore, it authorized the organization and financing of family-farm-development corporations whereby the poor would not be pushed from agricultural pursuits because of intense competition for their land. These corporations, serving as cooperatives, offer the potential for constructing a microeconomy capitalized by this title (see Toner, 1977). No mention is made of personal transportation as a factor inhibiting economic stability or growth.

Housing and Urban Development Act of 1965

Title X of this act provided mortgage insurance in subdivision development where none existed before. It represented the initial congressional encouragement for large-scale developments. The mortgage insurance program clause was narrowly drawn and infrequently used, however. During the congressional hearings the following year on subsequent amendments, "new communities" were proposed by the Council of State Governments as a deterrent to urban sprawl: "[This act] marked the beginning of Congressional concern to involve states and other public agencies in large-scale land development" (Stubbs, 1976, p. 11). While the act explicitly mandated urban containment, it recognized immense deficiencies in rural infrastructure, such as in housing settlements, water resources delivery systems, and recreation facilities.

Appalachian Redevelopment Act of 1965

This act was the first major piece of legislation to tackle transportation problems in sparsely populated areas on a broad regional basis. It focused on human problems relating to the impact of immobility on the quality of life — as much as it did on enhancing commercial and industrial development. It provided for construction and operation of a highway network that would be safe, speedy, and conducive to social and recreational development as well as attractive to economic interests.

The purpose of this enactment was to invest public funds in an economic area that traditionally lagged behind the rest of the country. Its intent was to solve the basic, underlying problems of the Appalachian region (*U.S. Code:* PL 89–4, Vol. 1, 1966). It was the first attempt, beyond the Tennessee Valley Authority, to draw together a workable multistate economic planning and development arrangement under the aegis of a regional commission (Whisman, 1970b). While the House Committee on Public Works declared that public investments from this act would produce unquestioned national benefits, its focus evidently was geographic in nature.

The most essential program for future Appalachian development was an adequate highway system (*U.S. Code:* PL 89–4, Vol. 2, 1966). Without such a system to join the regular federal systems, remoteness and isolation would continue to hinder the development of these areas.

The original act authorized the construction of 2,350 miles of primary roads. Additionally, and a salient feature for rural reaches, the act authorized 1,000 miles of local access roads to service development sites in the more severely rugged terrain near the backwaters of the eastern rivers tributary system. Furthermore, it stated that the access roads should be designed for servicing job-creating activities, offering prospects of long-range employment to Appalachian workers. Significantly, the program would be funded from new appropriations based on a federal/state formula of 70/30 percent. There would be no reliance on the Highway Trust Fund. Although a small section of the act was devoted to other forms and modes of transportation, no mention was made of personal transit or other vehicles to carry workers to their jobs.

Urban Mass Transportation Act of 1966

The purpose of this act was to extend grant authorization under the Urban Mass Transportation Act of 1964. When reporting the Senate bill for this act out for passage, the Committee on Housing in the Banking and Currency Committee justified further federal financial assistance by comparing the cost of highway construction in and around the country's cities with a substantially reduced cost of mass transit construction to accomplish the same purpose. The committee report succinctly stated that fare box revenues alone could not support the type of programs required to serve the public. In considering the poor financial condition of the cities, no alternative appeared likely except to seek further financial assistance from the federal government. References were also made to the necessity for federal financial participation with cities and towns of all sizes to provide improved transit facilities and equipment to meet public transportation needs. Thus capital grants were authorized for facilities and equipment, but not for operations.

The act also called for a major research program with demonstration projects to develop new systems created from radical new technologies (*U.S. Code:* PL 89–562, Vol. 2, 1967). This act made no mention of providing programs or systems for the rural poor.

Economic Opportunity Amendments of 1966

This act authorized the initiation of Operation Headstart. The intent was to expand the work created by the Office of Economic Opportunity, which was designed to help others help themselves. Under Title II, Part A, urban and rural Community Action programs were promulgated. Under these amendments a community was defined further to include any area sufficiently homogeneous in character to be appropriate for an attack on poverty. The determination of such an area was to be made without regard for boundaries or political subdivisions (*U.S. Code:* PL 89–794, Vol. 3, 1967).

A national scheme was not intended; rather, a regional or local orientation considering political and legal constraints was to be the determinant. A provision was added to ensure maximum resource utilization by efficient use of such funds. This measure necessitated taking full advantage of existing facilities to house Community Action projects. However, no mention was made of using public school buses for transit.

Title III wrote in special programs to combat poverty in rural areas. Limits on loans to low-income rural families were raised from $2,500 to $3,000. Most important, the amendments expanded coverage to rural non-farm poor individuals, who comprise the majority of the rural poverty population, rather than limiting it to farmers.

Title IV, dealing with work experience and training, blended manpower development and social services "wherever feasible" into a coordinated activity. Supplemental funds allowed for work-connected expenses, such as travel, supplies, or uniforms. The standard of sufficiency was the full amount of the state's relevant definition of needed assistance. The amendment authorized programs to make funds available for travel, supported by precedents for this expense, but offered no vehicle or system for delivery to the journey-to-work commuter or trainee.

Appalachian Regional Development Act Amendments of 1967

Title V amendments provided for departures from categorical federal assistance to a comprehensive development program tailored to the peculiar needs of a region (*U.S. Code:* PL 80–103, Vol. 2, 1968).

Under Title II of the act, amendments were enacted to the Public Works and Economic Development Act of 1965. The amendments authorized increasing highway mileage limitations for the main corridors and local accesses by approximately 15% and 20%, respectively. The minority argued that under the Appalachian program and the Public Works programs, very little money had been used to open new areas for development; rather, it had been used primarily to improve existing highways. But John Whisman (1970a), representative of the Appalachian Regional Commission, posited that Appalachia's commission had been successful, while the other Title V commissions had not, because it focused on development tied to highway construction. He asserted that the other commissions concentrated too much on program planning and too little on implementation.

Economic Opportunity Amendments of 1967

Section 123(a) of the Economic Opportunity Amendments of 1967 authorizes financial assistance in urban and rural areas where necessary for comprehensive work and training programs. Such programs include, among other activities, (1) programs to provide part-time employment, on-the-job training, and useful work experience for students from low-income families in need of earnings to permit them to resume or maintain attendance in school; (2) employment centers and mobile employment service units to provide recruitment, counseling, and placement services conveniently located in urban *or* rural areas and easily accessible to the most disadvantaged; and (3) programs to provide incentives and reimbursements to private employers to train or hire unemployed or low-income persons. The incentives include payments that permit employers to provide employees residing in such areas with transportation to and from work or to reimburse needy employees for such transportation (*U.S. Code:* PL 90–222, Vol. 1, 1968).

Title II provides for Community Action programs. Its basic purpose is to focus all available local, state, federal, and private resources more directly on the goal of motivating and enabling low-income families and individuals in rural and urban areas to acquire the skills and knowledge needed for secure employment and self-sufficiency. This title specifically enunciates a policy to provide for basic health care, education, vocational training, and employment opportunities to enable the poor living in rural America to remain there and become self-sufficient. Furthermore, the policy discourages the rural poor from migrating to urban areas since such migration is frequently not in the best interests of the poor and tends to further congest the already overcrowded slums and ghettos.

Section 102 emphasizes a comprehensive approach to overcome complex problems of the most severely disadvantaged in rural areas with high concentrations of underemployment and low income. Section 109 permits allowances and support to provide enrollees with funds necessary to meet their needs. Section 241 requires the extension of benefits to develop pilot and demonstration activities focused on problems specifically pertaining to rural poverty. In this act no mention is made of the need for public transportation. Concomitantly, Section 105 amends Title IV to emphasize that small-business concerns with a high proportion of low-income workers be given special attention on investment incentives. Although not specifically stated, a combination of these programs could provide for demonstration projects that would offer journey-to-work transportation options (*U.S. Code:* PL 90–222, Vol. 2, 1968).

Housing and Urban Development Act of 1968

Title VI amends the Comprehensive Planning Section of the Housing Act of 1954. Section 601 of the 1968 Act extends the Section 701 urban planning activity — commonly known as the "3C process" — to facilitate *compre-*

hensive planning for rural development, including *coordinated* transportation systems, on a *continuing* basis. Provisions are made for municipalities with populations of less than 50,000 for counties regardless of population size, for economic development districts designated under Title IV of the Public Works and Economic Development Act of 1965, for the various Title V commissions established by the Appalachian Regional Development Act of 1965, and for local development districts certified under Section 301 of the latter act for entire areas or small municipalities within the Appalachian region. Planning assistance under this act includes comprehensive survey preparation and/or the resolving of traffic congestion problems, the facilitation of the circulation of people and goods, and the reduction of transportation needs.

Section 702 of the Urban Mass Transportation Act of 1964 is amended, also, to define the term *mass transportation*. The definition includes transportation by bus, rail, or other conveyance, either publicly or privately owned, that provides general or special service to the public on a regular or continuing basis over prescribed routes. The amendment specifically excludes school buses or charter service. Additionally, no specific mention is made of rural transportation problems, although capital grants for special service from ghettos to specific workplaces are authorized (*U.S. Code:* PL 90–448, Vol. 1, 1969).

The committee minority pointed to the fact that, contrary to popular opinion, most of the country's substandard housing was not located in the deteriorated slum neighborhoods of our major cities, but instead prevailed in our rural areas or small towns. Further, they noted that more than 52% of all dilapidated housing units were in open rural country or in small towns containing a population of less than 2,500, compared with 24% of such units located in cities of over 50,000 people. Additionally, 64% of the non-dilapidated units found deficient in plumbing facilities were located in rural and small places.

Additionally, Title IV requires "an 'overall development plan' conforming to areawide considerations (including rural) with the provision of a substantial amount of low- and moderate-income housing" (Stubbs, 1976, p. 11). Furthermore, loan guarantees replaced mortgage insurance up to 90% of the amount; land and development costs obtained a greater proportion of funds; more efficient community facilities and infrastructure commanded implementation; open space programs gained prominent recognition; and advanced planning techniques and policy innovations resulted from the enactment. Apparently policymakers were becoming aware that rural living for the poor may be no less costly than urban living (*U.S. Code:* PL 90–448).

Housing and Urban Development Act of 1970

In contrast to its focus in the previous two decades, congressional interest in community development had shifted by 1970 to a pervasive, sound balance between rural and urban America (Stubbs, 1976, p. 11). Title VII under the 1970 Housing and Urban Development Act provided for congressional commitment to the "rational, orderly, efficient, and economic growth, development, and redevelopment of our states, metropol[es], cities, counties, towns, and communities in predominantly rural areas." Thus, the act enunciates preparation of a national growth policy, a policy never before considered. This title "mandates the biennial preparation of a National Urban Growth Policy . . . to foster planning and provides a policy framework to encourage balanced growth patterns" (Stubbs, 1976, p. 12). Moreover, Congress endorsed several well-planned, diversified, and economically sound new communities. The plans for such communities were to include protection of the environment; realization of potential growth in *"micropoles," small towns, rural communities*, and older central cities; provision for substantial amounts of low-income housing; and integration of social planning by innovating social programs for community development, which implicitly suggests the need for spatial mobility among the rural poor. Provisions stated in more recent legislation began to address the spatial and temporal immobility problem of the rural poor.

Urban Mass Transportation Assistance Act of 1970

Section 8 of the Urban Mass Transportation Act of 1964 is amended by adding a new section authorizing the planning and design of mass transportation facilities to meet special needs of the elderly and handicapped. This amendment is the first in a series of amendments that focus on a particular interest group. Section 16(a) clearly states that elderly and handicapped persons have the same right as other persons to utilize mass transportation facilities and services. It directs that in planning and designing mass transportation facilities and services, special consideration be given to the needs of elderly and handicapped persons. All federal programs offering assistance in transportation should contain provisions implementing this policy.

Section 16(b) authorizes grants and loans for the specific purpose of assisting states and local public bodies and agencies in providing the special needs mentioned above. Section 16(d) in this act defines specifically the term *handicapped persons* to mean persons who, in varying degrees, are incapable of reaching transportation services. Section 9 authorizes research into the feasibility of providing federal assistance to help defray operating costs of mass transportation companies in urban areas (*U.S. Code:* PL 91-453, Vol. 1, 1971). Although labeled "urban," several federal grants have been made to smaller cities; twenty-seven were given to municipalities of less than 25,000 inhabitants. A growing recognition that smaller cities have been hit hardest with soaring costs and declining budgets has been evidenced among the Congressional Banking and Currency Committee members in their hearings with smaller city mayors and county officials. This act served as the basis for moving funds from grants and loans for capital expenditures to continuing operating expenditures (*U.S. Code:* PL 91-453, Vol. 2, 1971). However, no mention is made of programs for the rural poor who may be immobile.

Rural Development Act of 1972

The goal of this act was to attain more balanced population and economic growth, with equal intent to reverse the continual migration to the cities by making rural America a better place in which to work and live. Section 106 amends the Consolidated Farmers Home Administration Act of 1961 to extend all programs to cities and towns with populations under 5,500 (*U.S. Code:* PL 92-418, Vol. 2, 1973). Section 109 expands the definitions of *rural* and *rural area* to include all the territory of a state that is not within the outer boundary of any city containing 50,000 or more inhabitants and immediate adjacent urbanizing areas with densities of over 100 persons per square mile. Variations regarding the size of the community do exist depending on other specific activity criteria (*U.S. Code:* PL 92-418, Vol. 1, 1973).

More important than the enactment of the operational definition is the rationale posited by the Congressional Committee on Agriculture and Forestry as reported in one legislative document. The committee defined some of the issues by comparing rural to urban situations in terms of variables such as substandard housing, per capita income, and employment for rural residents, among others. The report states that the crux of the problem is generally poorer conditions in rural America than in urban America. These conditions have led to migration and to the chronic problems now existing in the poorer areas of most cities. The report also mentions the remoteness and clumsiness of the federal government in responding to state and local needs:

> State and local governments are frequently too impoverished or too fragmented to undertake the necessary planning and development activities. Their problems

are accentuated by the fact that widely dispersed rural population means a higher expenditure per person for most government programs. [*U.S. Code:* PL 92–418, Vol. 2, 1973, pp. 3148–49]

Apparently, the adapted version evolving from the Conference Committee focused only on assistance to facilitate industrial development, which was intended to provide employment for rural residents. Also, loans were authorized for "essential community facilities," which means that loans would be available to associations that provided facilities needed for the orderly development of a rural community. Although no specific sections focused on transportation, this legislation, along with Section 147 of the 1973 Federal-Aid Highway Act, set the stage for rural transportation programs.

Federal-Aid Highway Act of 1973

This act broadened the scope in transportation activities from construction solely of high-speed highway facilities to several mobility services. Several sections of previous legislation have been amended. First of all, under Title I, in addition to authorizing almost equal sums for rural areas as for urban, Section 104(a)(2) authorizes use of the heretofore protected monies contained in the Highway Trust Fund established in Section 209(f)(1) of the Highway Revenue Act of 1956. Second, Section 105(2) defines the urban/rural population delineation at 5,000 inhabitants as designated by the Bureau of the Census. Third, Section 121 amends the public transportation section (142) of the 1956 act to finance equipment purchases (buses) for use on federal systems facilities. Fourth, Section 122 amends Section 143 of the 1956 act by changing the status of "demonstration projects" for economic growth center development highways to continuing activities commensurate with any other project on the federal aid system. Fifth, Section 124 amends the 1956 act by adding a new section to encourage the development and improvement of exclusive pedestrian walkways in conjunction with highway rights of way, along with bicycle paths, where no motorized vehicles would be permitted to operate (*U.S. Code:* PL 93–87, Vol. 1, 1974). Sixth, public mass transportation studies were to be performed by the Transportation Department to assess transit needs and analyze contemporary funding mechanisms. Finally, a great rural public transportation demonstration program was established under Section 147. Specifically, it encourages the development, improvement, and use of public mass transportation systems that operate vehicles on highways for the transportation of passengers within rural areas in order to enhance the access of rural populations to employment and public services. Congress authorized appropriations of $30 million for a period of two fiscal years ending June 30, 1976, of which $20 million was allocated to carry out demonstration projects for public mass transportation in rural areas. Projects eligible for federal funds under this section include facilities to serve bus and other public transportation passengers and the purchase of passenger equipment other than rolling stock for fixed rail.

In a more concentrated area, this 1973 enactment under Title III in Section 301(g) 16(b) amends the Urban Mass Transportation Act of 1964. It provides for grants and loans amounting to 80% of project costs. Subsection 16(b)(1) authorizes such loans and grants to states and local bodies for special needs of elderly and handicapped persons, while subsection 16(b)(2) authorizes similar funds to private nonprofit corporations if such services are unavailable, insufficient, or inappropriate within a public agency.

The act provides a framework for cost-effective transportation for the poor seeking or traveling to work.

Housing and Community Development Act of 1974

Under Title VIII, Section 813 amends the Urban Mass Transportation Act of 1964, whereby no federal financial assistance will be provided for the purchase of transit buses unless the applicant agrees not to engage in charter bus operations outside the urban area within which it provides regularly scheduled transit services (*U.S. Code:* PL 93–382, Vol. 1, 1975). The reason for this restriction, as written in the Federal-Aid Highway Act of 1973, is to prohibit competition for private bus operators outside the area. The above section, 164(a), was added to this act to permit grantees the opportunity to offer charter service to the public where no other service currently exists (*U.S. Code:* PL 93–382, Vol. 3, 1975, p. 4358).

National Mass Transportation Act of 1974

This act was passed for the purpose of inhibiting the reduction of public transportation service. The amendments authorize the first subsidy by the federal government to be used for operating grants. The subsidies are directly aimed at assistance for the poor and the elderly. The enactment is consequent to what the congressional committees regard as the apparent inequities of unreasonably high fares (*U.S. Code:* PL 93–503, Vol. 3, 1975).

Section 203(2) mandates that the cities be selected from places of varying sizes. Of signal importance, Congress directed the Urban Mass Transportation Administration (UMTA) to set aside $500 million of Section 3 capital grant funds for use in nonurbanized areas (*U.S. Code:* PL 93–503, vol. 1, 1975).

Regional Development Act of 1975

Title V of this act, cited as the Appalachian Regional Development Act Amendments of 1975, establishes seven Regional Action Planning Commissions comprising all or parts of thirty-one states (*U.S. Code:* PL 94–188, Vol. 2, 1976). The report states that the major purpose of the commission programs is to respond to the goals of "narrowing the income gap, creating more jobs, and increasing education levels." Since the regions typically are rural, containing widely spaced small towns with low population density, the Senate Committee on Public Works expanded the program authority of the commissions in the fields of energy, transportation, education, and health. The concern about energy and transportation subsequent to the short-fall of petroleum and the attendant price increase narrowly focuses on the problem of transportation rate regulation. As an adjunct to this act, under the heading of "Other Provisions," the Appalachian Commission is directed to give special attention to studies and demonstrations for the improvement of rural public transportation. These activities are to be implemented under Section 147 of the Federal-Aid Highway Act of 1973 or any other authority that would permit such studies. Ironically, the act authorized a decrease of 200 local access miles for an additional 200 developmental highway corridor miles in a region that formerly was not part of the original Appalachian network when the corridors were established.

Surface Transportation Act of 1978

Section 146 provides for measures to encourage car-pooling opportunities by identifying potential riders *other than* the elderly and handicapped. Subsection (d) establishes technical assistance mechanisms through state and local governments while removing local barriers to increase participation. Subsection (e), on the other hand, prohibits the use of grant money for the purchase or lease of vehicles for such a program (*U.S. Code:* PL 95–599, Vol. 1, 1978).

Section 18(d) makes available a "Formula Grant Program for Other Urbanized Areas." Subsection (d) allows only a 15% contribution to recipients for technical assistance, while subsection (e) affords 50% and 80% for operation and construction costs, respectively. This legislation, like so many of its precedents, does not address the issue of carlessness.

Section 323 is amended under Subsection 22(a) "to make grants for the initiation, continuation, or improvement of intercity bus service for residents in rural areas . . ." not located within urbanized areas. This subsection specifically excludes local service operating off the main highways.

This prohibition exacerbates the obvious for micropoles and hinterlands. Comments concerning small-area budget deficiencies in governments and their treasuries are stated above in the Rural Development Act of 1972. Much like the drunkard who searches under the street lamp for the keys he lost in the dark, many states, with the concurrence of UMTA, are performing intercity bus travel studies to determine rural work-trip-commuting needs for public transportation service (Tyner, 1980). The major problem, as noted above, is getting to the highway from the backwater reaches, ridges, and hollows, rather than merely flagging the scheduled carrier as it passes a designated point on the main highway (Tarter, 1976). Additionally, rural systems seeking to expand their services to include work trips under Section 18 have found that the new regulations complicate the process. Section 13(c) of the original 1964 Urban Mass Transportation Act (U.S. Department of Transportation: PL 88-365, 1965), which related to minimum wage, union contracts, and other labor laws such as driver schedules, contravenes the mission of hiring drivers from the ranks of rural would-be resident workers otherwise resigned to the ranks of the nonemployed (McKelvey, 1979).

While this program is the first comprehensive attempt by the Federal Department of Transportation to assist states and local government units to meet the transportation needs of rural work commuters, requirements for ramps and lifts to facilitate the physically handicapped lowers the program's probability of success. This projection is based on cost alone; a fully equipped vehicle with all the attendant accoutrements increases the price at least fourfold (National Rural Center, 1979).

Although the act is fraught with prohibitions, restrictions, and constraints, this new USDOT program offers a unique opportunity to improve coordination through more efficient use of existing transportation services (U.S. Department of Transportation, 1979). Prior to its passage, a study by the Administration on Aging in 1977 identified over eighty programs that were in process to facilitate mobility for the elderly and handicapped. Needless to say, states Brooks (1976–1977), many wasteful overlaps of vehicles and personal services prevailed. This kind of redundancy was not limited to urban areas, however; a 1977 GAO audit (CED 77–119) reported that 114 different federal programs existed to provide transportation services in rural areas.

As a consequence of the Section 18 enactment and the White House

Rural Development Initiatives (Bivens, 1979), the U.S. Departments of Transportation and Agriculture joined together in 1981 to innovate an approach for rural public transportation advocacy. They agreed to initiate a coordinated action by placing a USDA traffic management specialist in each Federal Highway Administration regional office to provide assistance to users of transport services in small counties and rural areas by adjusting to various reform measures. Additionally, the interagency mechanisms of the Rural Development Task Forces within the Federal Regional Councils, established by Executive Order of the President No. 11647, dated February 10, 1972, will assist state efforts to aid rural and small community citizens. To facilitate this assistance, a full Farmers Home Administration (FmHA) staff member, rural development coordinator, will serve as FmHA's liaison between the White House Staff (of the Carter Administration) and state officials responsible for rural policy and issues (Bivens, 1979–1981).

Housing and Community Development Act of 1979

Section 104(a)(2)(B) provides for alleviating "pockets of poverty" in communities with populations of less than 50,000, including nonmetropolitan areas in (any) state, where 70% of the residents earn incomes below 80% of the area's median family income (*U.S. Code:* PL 96–153, Vol. 1, 1979). The key criteria determining eligibility include a comparative degree of physical and commercial deterioration among eligible areas, a substantial contribution to the enhancement of the physical and economic development of an area, and direct benefits to low- and moderate-income families residing in designated areas. Section 509 provides for minimal housing to migrant farm workers under Title V. Under "Farm Labor Housing Assistance," applicants are eligible for 90% of development costs. These funds do not go to the poor residents themselves, but rather to developers who must construct safe and weatherproof housing.

Rural Policy Development Act of 1980

The significance of this act is demonstrated by the creation of an undersecretary in the Department of Agriculture for small-community and rural development. This new secretary will co-chair an interagency working group of policy officials. The other co-chairperson is to be the president's special assistant for intergovernmental affairs (National Rural Center, 1980). The enactment mandates preparation of a comprehensive rural development strategy based on state, regional, and local needs, objectives, and plans (*U.S. Code:* PL 96-355, Vol. 1, 1980). The mandate adheres to the Carter Administration's policy implemented to enhance the development of rural areas and to improve the quality of rural life (Bivens, 1980-81).

Summary

The enactments cited above provide a chronological history of federal legislation over the past two decades pertaining to employment programs for the poor and attendant provisions intended to alleviate associated costs thought to be directly related to the journey to work and work-training trips. They also provide an anecdotal record of national policy and enactments of more than a decade and a half relating to mobility and accessibility for the disadvantaged — the poor, young, elderly, or handicapped — that would reduce work-commuter dependence on privately owned (householder) vehicles. It is quite evident, even with the fuel shortages and cost increases for owning and operating an automobile, that public transit such as minibuses and jitneys may not be a viable alternative in sparsely populated rural areas. "The absence of concentrations of users and captive riders found in larger urban areas makes rural bus service, both intra- and intercity, expensive to provide" (Getzels and Thurow, 1979, p. 224).

Although many micropoles — fifteen thousand of them — are located on or along intercity bus routes, they cannot generate enough traffic alone as origin or destination points to justify service for themselves. "Unfortunately, regularly scheduled services to these areas have deteriorated in recent years and the trend is expected to continue" (Levine, 1977, p. 120). Furthermore, an estimated 50% of micropoles containing populations of less than 10,000 people receive no intercity bus service at all (Goldschmidt, 1980). Moreover, "intercity transit . . . has the capability of serving *only a small portion* of the needs of a small town" (Getzels and Thurow, 1979, p. 225). As posited above, neither taxi nor paratransit is a viable, feasible alternative for long-distance rural work commutation.

As we have seen, the search through the legislation pertaining to housing, economic development, and transportation reveals a significant disparity between urban and rural problems as viewed by Congress. This disparity is no less prevalent in the few state legislatures that have begun to deal with the plight of the rural poor. The problem has been ignored by state and local policymakers and planning managers until the very recent past. For example, at the Conference on Statewide Transportation Planning (in which I was an active workshop participant), no attention was given to, nor mention made of, the problem of rural transit in small places.

The two workshops where this topic would have fit best did not address it among the stated objectives and listed issues. The first workshop — Systems Planning and Programming Methodology: [1974] Passenger Travel — focused on the identification and evaluation of techniques used to develop statewide multimodal transportation plans and programs for the movement of persons and goods. The second workshop —State and Regional Development — keyed on the identification of strategies being developed to address linkages between transportation planning and comprehensive development planning at state and regional levels. Although this conference was held during the zenith of the energy shortfall, few were cognizant of the subsequent impact on rural areas and, more specifically, on their poor residents.

STATE PROGRAMS

Discussions with several authorities throughout the research for this project revealed that, prior to the 1973 Federal-Aid Highway Act, virtually no rural public transportation operations existed. Reichart corroborates this finding:

> Relatively little operational experience currently exists from which we can draw to answer the questions of what types of services *are possible and desirable* in rural areas, *how* these services can most effectively be *organized* and *operated* and *how* these services can be *supported financially*. [Reichart, 1975, p. 157; italics added]

The seriousness of the problem in rural areas finally is being recognized by administrators and is reflected in the number of proposal submittals to acquire demonstration project funds. In 1976, the first year of the program, 350 proposals were submitted, requesting in excess of $120 million against a funding level of $9.65 million. However, the focus of the projects apparently was not on work-trip commuters. Of seven typical projects selected in as many states for discussion by Reichart, six were funded for the handicapped and elderly or for other social service types of system. In the seventh project, servicing three small towns with less than 5,000 inhabitants each, the clientele was not specified. Reichart affirms that FHWA holds the position that the states should obtain the *prime* authority and responsibility for providing nonurbanized areas with adequate public transportation service.

In short, public transportation in both urban and rural areas is about to experience severe service cuts. President Reagan already has asked for substantial cuts in the transportation infrastructure — particularly in mass transit. The Office of Management and Budget is leading the charge that the transit marketplace will prevail (Stockman, 1981). Concurrently, congressional and special interests are engaged in debate over subsidy cuts and fare box restructuring for existing urban systems. Transit lobbyists assert that the fare box alone is not the answer, while, simultaneously, audit trails of transit operations suggest more efficient management would mitigate operating deficits substantially ("MacNeil/Lehrer Report," 1981). Interviews were held during a forum with John Vialet, chief auditor of the General Accounting Office; Jack Gilstrap, manager of American Public Transit Associates; Senator Richard Lugar (R) of Indiana; and Congressman James Howard (D) of New Jersey. This group was debating the impending collapse of the Metropolitan Boston Transit Authority: Vialet asserted gross inefficiencies, while Gilstrap posited that public subsidy remains the only option.

Meanwhile, system after system is observed to be in some sort of financial trouble. For example, the city transit operation of Birmingham, Alabama, was shut down because of bankruptcy (Kuralt, 1981), and metropolitan system workers in Philadelphia went on strike with "no settlement in sight" (Kohn, 1981). All in all, given the Reagan Administration's objectives — which are in juxtaposition to those of advocates of public-funded mass transit — current conditions do not augur well for subsidized transportation.

A brief discussion of the rural experience in Georgia will illustrate the misplaced emphasis of its administrators. (For an analysis of individualized state programs, see Maggied, 1979, pp. 147–74.)

Georgia

The lack of focus on rural population sparsity was emphasized repeatedly by Ira Kaye (1977) during a conversation, and in a confirmation letter, while discussing the inaccessibility and immobility of the rural poor in Georgia, particularly in Atlanta's environs. He decried the fact that many metropolitan government officials neglect counties like Douglas, Gwinnett, and Rockdale, where more than two-thirds of their local population (1970 Census) lives in rural areas. Approximately 8% to 10% of the rural households in those counties are totally deprived of personal transportation — that is, they are carless.

Several studies conducted for various areas in the state of Georgia deal only with highway construction and the movement of vehicles, not with vehicle access. For example, in an early study by Lemly (1958), "accessibility" was discussed in relationship to driving on or near a piece of land. A decade later, a study by Wallace and Lemly (1969) used what the research team referred to as the "standard published economic indicators," which include population increase, labor force and employment trends, entry rates for new industry, increases in agricultural output, income growth, bank deposit increases, retail sales, and educational attainment. This study explored impacts on land use and existing business places, among other activities. A glaring omission in this economic impact study is any reference to the social impact of work-trip commuting or other travel. While comparisons were made for "before and after" conditions, no discussion concerned the quality of the work force or its members' ability to travel consistently to workplaces from their residences. In fact, even the land use map omitted any designation of the residential areas' land use.

A later study by Bates (1970) revealed an effort to include rural areas in the transportation planning process. Although the title "Comprehensive Planning for Rural Regions: A Case Study (The Slash Pine Experience)" indicates an all-encompassing study, the research focused only on developmental aspects of the region. Since the primary sources of trip data were "volume counts" — that is, roadway traffic checks of origin and destination by car — it is obvious that the mobility disadvantaged were omitted from the study.

A more recent study deals with the social impact of the construction of a developmental highway in a ten-county region of Appalachian North Georgia (Interplan, 1974). While the 1970 population of each county ranged between 3,600 and 31,000, the largest town in the region numbered slightly over 3,600 inhabitants. The size of these communities indicates that the county residuals, and thus the region's population, are highly rural. The study was quite extensive, and the research team did analyze regional commuting by employing a time-distance matrix that depicted the percentage of manufacturing industries that chose locations in Appalachia within ten to fifteen minutes' travel by auto. An important finding in the study is that a major source of income for the regional economy is generated by area residents commuting to employment places outside the region. In-commuters represent over 25% of the total labor force working in the region. Regional inhabitants account for 15% and 20% of the population that commutes to the Atlanta and Gainesville areas, respectively.

The researchers also note that at any point in time, commuting patterns reflect the spatial distribution of economic activities and residential development. Any changes in regional accessibility under the various alternative routes of the Appalachian Highway will produce changes in this spatial distribution and, therefore, in commuting patterns.

While the study relates to highway construction and its attendant benefits, it provides some valuable insights and information for substantiating that the basic assumption pertaining to spatial distribution and accessibility, applied to automobile owners, logically extends to the carless and other mobility disadvantaged. Whenever a facility or service is provided, it offers an element of mobility choice to the residents who have chosen rural living while avoiding the captivity of isolation. It also permits movement through uncongested traffic while allowing freedom to commute.

Many residents, as the study concludes, are satisfied and like their communities as they are. Few see the new highway as a threat to the small-town atmosphere. They hope to retain its existing physical and social attributes, even though they need better regional facilities. The same questions need to be asked of the poor who are unemployed and carless when it is recommended, legislated, and programmed that they relocate away from a familiar habitat to obtain work.

Only two rural transit studies have been authorized by the Georgia Department of Transportation. The initial study covered three regions: two located in northwest Appalachian Georgia, and the third situated in eastern Georgia on the Coastal Plains. The second study focused on a single region along the Coastal Crescent.

The multiregional study performed by Kimley-Horn (1975a) intended to generate a capital grants program that would provide special transportation services to meet the needs of the rural elderly and handicapped under authorization by Section 16(b)(2) of the Urban Mass Transportation Act of 1964, as amended. The report covers the Central Savannah River APDC, North Georgia APDC, and Coosa Valley APDC. Further, it was to serve as the Planning and Development Program for only eight counties in the three APDCs. The report is unclear, however. The maps and tables that illustrate the data depict all the Central Savannah River and North Georgia counties, but only three counties from Coosa Valley. While a set of data from the study shows rural target group totals for various counties, it is difficult to ascertain how the values were derived. Because of its lack of clarity, this report proved to be of little value in this literature search.

The single-region study was undertaken by Kimley-Horn (1976) to provide the basis for an application to the Federal Highway Administration for capital and operating assistance through demonstration funds under Section 147 of the Federal-Aid Highway Act of 1973.

The study concentrated on three of the eight counties in the Coastal Area Planning and Development Commission. The initial analysis focused on programs for the transportation disadvantaged — including the elderly and the handicapped. One can conclude from the above that the Coastal Plains study was not intended exclusively for the elderly and handicapped, but was more comprehensive. To corroborate this conclusion, the study included a survey to determine (a) where the major employers in the study region were located and (b) the work-trip characteristics of their employees.

The report states that the results were considered statistically invalid because of a varied frequency of responses from the employers. Two counties elicited no responses, and a third (Chatham County) received responses from only 11% of those surveyed. The rationale of the study team is questioned here; the firms sampled in the "no-response" counties numbered one each. "No-response" refers to sample counties where employers were surveyed and none returned their survey instruments. Chatham County contains Savannah City, with a population exceeding 100,000, which should serve as an adequate statistical universe even with an 11% response. Additionally, in the subsequent analysis the data are aggregated and displayed as a "Seven-County Study Area," which does not comport to the three-county region described above nor to the eight-county journey-to-work study.

A more recent study "GAMTRAN" (Georgia Mountains APDC, 1976) was undertaken to develop the plan necessary to qualify for grant funds authorized under Section 147 of the Federal-Aid Highway Act of 1973. The study was designed as a comprehensive approach that would encompass all existing transportation programs in the thirteen-county Georgia Mountains Planning and Development District. The district plan proposed to meet the special needs of today's intercounty and intracounty commuters, the poor, the elderly, and the handicapped, as well as all citizens of the region. Demand-response service to social service agencies and to the general public in rural areas as well as the city of Gainesville (25,000 population) would be provided. In the Georgia Mountains Transportation study, an important component included the journey-to-work commuters.

This study was a departure from previous rural, regional, transit, or transportation studies. It attempted, to a large degree successfully, to identify the transportation needs of the rural poor. The data for the Georgia Mountains Transportation proposal correspond to the variables selected for the methodology of my own research, as indicated in Chapter 1.

Apparently, the project under study was not a total success. Several times during the project, the authorized carrier petitioned the Georgia Public Service Commission (Bush, 1977–1978) for various "route abandonments" that proved to be unprofitable in the Georgia Mountains project. The particular routes that proved to be troublesome were those designed to carry work commuters at times beyond the typical 8:00 A.M. to 5:00 P.M. work period. While some of the extended time transits were abandoned, most transits to service social agency programs are expected to continue (Dayton, 1978).

CONCLUSION

Based on the literature review, little was found to suggest that the rural poor, particularly the nonworkers, have been the focus of transportation programs. Transportation as a function developed from objectives related to physical commodity movement rather than human community transit. Mobility of the rural economically disadvantaged is ignored almost totally. Despite the various programs formulated in the legislative enactments, the evidence reveals policymakers' insensitivity about the need of the isolated poor for accessibility and mobility to job sites in a very mobile society. Most studies relating to rural transportation utilize methodologies that are suspect. If they have dealt with economic growth, which should include the enhancement of the rural resident's income level, they have focused on either increased commodity movement or faster speeds generated by improved, unimpeded, limited-access highways; cost savings to the firm dominate the findings. If they have focused on the transits of people, social services emerge as the central theme, dominated by handicapped and elderly issues. In cases of manpower development and public works programs, *funding* for relocation expenses for migrants was included in the package, but problems of door-to-door conveyance for commuters was all but ignored. In the final analysis, "masses" do not live in rural areas. The sparsity of population dictates the dispersed nature of rural trips, and the trip *needs* are basic to the understanding of rural transportation problems (Saltzman, 1975; Kaye, 1976a). Neither conventional urban public transportation, nor weekly eight-to-five transportation programs, nor suggested off-peak school buses, mail buggies, or social service volunteers provide a viable alternative to transport America's rural mobility disadvantaged.

This chapter on federal legislation presented a synopsis following a comprehensive examination to ascertain whether legislation was enacted and programs were innovated to provide viable transportation systems for residents of rural America who require mobility to obtain accessibility to their employment. Because of the complexities in implementing and operating transportation systems, the dynamics in commuter behavior, the range of personal income levels, the dispersion of employment activity, and the intricacies and vagaries of public policy, which are elusive at best, it was felt that lengthy, exhaustive documentation of the legislative literature was necessary to explicate fully the highlights of the issues. More important, the federal enactments were synopsized and state activities summarized to reveal that the myriad and diverse foci missed a significant target population that should be apparent, if not obvious, to all policy analysts dealing with the problem of rural mobility. Equally important, it uncovered an absence of legislation that, if enacted, could provide continual programs for work-commuter-oriented public transportation. Moreover, it supports the early assertion in this research of benign neglect regarding the rural poor.

4 FACTOR ANALYSIS AND EVALUATION OF WORKER MOBILITY VARIABLES

As stated earlier, a factor analysis was performed to determine whether the mobility/personal income/work activity model was valid. The key variables initially assumed to be relevant were assessed to discern the variables anticipated to be most significant in relation to the three-parameter model. A final selection reduced the original variable set from sixteen to the following eight:

Variable Number	Variable
1	Level, Median Family Income: 1976
2	Incidence, Out-County Work Commuters: 1970
3	Rate, Labor Force Participation: 1976
4	Incidence, Household Automobile Unavailability: 1970
5	Incidence, Unpaved County Roads: 1976
6	Incidence, Poverty Families per Area: 1976
7	Incidence, Small Communities per Area: 1975
8	Designation, Rural/Urban Work Commuter Counties: 1972

Variable Number	Computer Descriptor
1	MDFMY
2	CMUTRS
3	LFPR
4	CRLES
5	UNPVD
6	Y < $8K
7	%U < 5K
8	RUK

Definitions for these variables were given in Chapter 1.

The analysis of the eight variables was run at two geopolitical levels: (a) Georgia's 18 Area Planning and Development Commissions (APDCs) and (b) Georgia's 159 counties. To preserve the sample size, urban counties were not delimited from the data set for the factor analysis. The extracted factor constraints fell into a single pattern for the APDCs and into three patterns for the counties.

FINDINGS: APDCs

The analysis of the eight variables applied to the 18 APDCs produced a single factor. The coefficients in the correlation matrix are significant at the 5% level in all but four of the thirty-six observations. For the APDCs, any $r > .456$ is significant at the 0.05 level; any $r > .575$ is significant at the 0.01 level. Over 61% of the variance proportion in the variables that overlap with this factor is explained by the communalities obtained from it after six iterations. Additionally, the extracted factor pattern indicates some heavy loadings by the variables on this single factor. The factor scores for the APDCs indicate little deviation from the mean other than in the Atlanta region.

Correlation Matrix

The coefficients in the correlation matrix construct shown in Table 4.1 reveal some interesting relationships. For expediency, the report on the findings is grouped in deciles except at significance levels.

Table 4.1   Correlation Coefficients of the Eight-Variable Factor Analysis on the Eighteen APDCs in Georgia

| | Factor Correlations | | | | | | | |
Variable	1	2	3	4	5	6	7	8
1. MDFMY	1.000							
2. CMUTRS	+.572	1.000						
3. LFPR	+.552	+.420	1.000					
4. CRLES	−.786	−.248	−.722	1.000				
5. UNPVD	−.836	−.763	−.554	+.564	1.000			
6. Y<$8K	−.951	−.605	−.513	+.708	+.897	1.000		
7. %U<5K	−.707	−.322	−.341	+.592	+.529	+.660	1.000	
8. RUK	+.655	+.554	+.475	−.518	−.615	−.633	−.827	1.000

Source: University of Georgia, Geography Department (1979).

Median Family Income (MDFMY).   Family income is significant at the 5% level with all variables tested. As would be expected, this variable has an almost perfect, although negative, correlation to poverty, Y<$8K: MDFMY (6,1), in the highest decile group. It is interesting to note that these two variables are significant at the 1% level for almost every case; the two exceptions nearly meet this criterion. It is also striking that MDFMY correlates next best, negatively, with unpaved county roads, UNPVD (5,1). This relationship may be explained by the poorness of the county residents, who do not contribute much to the tax base necessary for obtaining apportionments for county road contracts administered by the state. The relationship appears valid by a companion correlation between UNPVD and Y<$8K (6,5), although it is diametrically (positively) opposed.

The next decile group observed is the relationship to carlessness, CRLES (4,1), and small communities, %U<5K (7,1), respectively. As expected, both are negatively correlated. It is believed that the reason MDFMY and CRLES are not more closely related is that income recipients obtain transportation means other than by their own automobile availability for income purposes. In the case of %U<5K, some small communities are selective by virtue of their high income and, conversely, contribute to lesser correlation than might be expected in typical small, rural communities.

In the next decile level, the only relationship that resulted was with the rural/urban work commuter designation, RUK (8,1). This interrelationship differs almost diametrically from the MDFMY:%U<5K situation by resulting in a positive correlation. The most that can be ascribed to this relationship is that urban dwellers generally receive higher incomes.

I expected the next decile group, while it is significant, to have stronger interrelationships to MDFMY. Moreover, the variables LFPR and CMUTRS, (3,1) and (2,1), were expected to have strong relationships. Out-county commuters, CMUTRS, generally travel to work for higher income than they can receive in their own county, but (2,1) indicates that other factors may impinge upon that condition. One of those factors may be that within the universe of Georgia's numerous counties, where surpluses of workers exist because jobs are not available, CMUTRS must "take what they can get" in regard to their personal income. Much of the same analysis can be applied to the relationship of MDFMY to work activity, LFPR (3,1). In rural counties jobs are not as readily available as in urban counties and, therefore, a lesser correlation results. Additionally, and possibly more importantly, the working share of inhabitants in an area does not necessarily have any relationship to the MDFMY level.

Out-County Work Commuters (CMUTRS). This variable presented some surprising results. First of all, of the four coefficients in the thirty-six-cell correlation matrix that were not significant at the 5% level, three were interrelated with this variable: CRLES (4,2), %U < 5K (7,2), and LFPR (3,2). While the %U < 5K: CMUTRS would be difficult to explain even with a highly structured investigation, it was expected that work activity would correlate highly and positively with out-county commutation. Concomitantly, it was expected that work activity would correlate highly, but negatively, with automobile unavailability. I am at a loss to explain its insignificance. The remaining three observations are significant at the 5% level, with only one (8,2) exceeding the 1% level. The highest-level relationship is between UNPVD and CMUTRS: (5,2). It is not surprising that high levels of poor facilities would impinge upon work-trip commuter patterns. The next level reveals a negative relationship (7,2) that was expected to be greater: Y < $8K with CMUTRS. Part of this nonfulfillment of expectation may be attributed to the disparity in the time frames of the variables. The values for the poverty variable were developed for 1976, whereas for commuters they were developed in 1970. More important, however, the rationale for why the poor travel to work activity or choose to remain at home is part of the decision process that is not understood well. Moreover, it is not within the scope of this research. The third significant observation, RUK (8,2), was expected by its very nature to correlate almost perfectly. No explanation is apparent, and without further investigation no cause-and-effect relationship can be given.

Work Activity (LFPR). Within the five other observations for the work activity variable, the remaining insignificant correlation, %U < 5K:LFPR

(7,3), along with (3,2) already discussed, is not significant at the 5% level. Its negativeness is explicable by the fact that small communities generally do not have large employment activity bases; thus it is logical that a large number of small communities with low income would experience high rates of nonworkers. But looking back to MDFMY:LFPR (3,1), we see that the correlation observed is not relatively significant at the 1% level but is significant at the 5% level. Thus the work activity variable may require more extensive investigation for understanding its role in the APDCs. The highest-level correlation to LFPR is with CRLES (4,3). Although its negativeness is not as high as I had expected, this finding strongly supports the hypothesis set forth in the early stages of this research. To further strengthen the hypothesis, this is the only relationship between LFPR and the other selected variables that attains significance at the 1% level. The next decile group contains UNPVD:LFPR (5,3) and Y < $8K:LFPR (6,3); both are insignificant at the 1% level, but do meet the level of 5%. The former negativeness may be explained by the inability of remote, inconvenienced inhabitants to traverse poor road facilities in their transits to work, while the latter may be explained by the lack of funds to purchase the means for work transits. The final significant relationship to LFPR, a positive one, is with RUK (8,3). The coefficient meets the 5% significance level and is, incidentally, the lowest coefficient for RUK (8,n). (All but two others meet the 1% confidence limits, and those two — (8,2) and (8,4) — nearly approach the 1% significance level.)

Automobile Unavailability (CRLES). This variable — which was the initial underlying concern in the cause/effect relationship of this research — presents some interesting, as well as significant, findings. While only one of the coefficients discussed above, (4,2), does not meet the 5% significance level, only two are significant at the 1% level. Beyond the low CRLES:CMUTR coefficient (4,2), the remaining relationships split evenly into two decile groups of three each. In the upper group, two coefficients discussed above, (4,1) and (4,3), are negative correlations. The third in this group, Y < $8K:CRLES, is a positive correlation, as was expected. It is reasonable to assume that poverty level families would maintain a higher incidence of carless households. In the lower decile group, two of the coefficients reveal positive correlations: UNPVD:CRLES (5,4) (this coefficient nearly approaches the 1 percent significance level), and %U < 5K:CRLES (7,4). While all the elements of the former are not understood fully, it seems reasonable that poor people who live in poor areas and are unable to obtain automobiles in an automobile-oriented society are less able to procure public goods in the form of paved roads. Regarding the former positive correlation, a similar rationale follows: small communities with low population bases may be compact, self-contained units that foster the walk mode, personal rapid transit, or some demand-responsive method. This assumption is highly unlikely, however; most of the literature reviewed and discussions held with state, APDC, and local officials for this research indicate that the rural poor who have no automobiles do without solely for economic reasons. The final coefficient (8,4) in this group reveals a negative correlation. It indicates that more carless households are situated in rural areas than in urban ones (see Table 1.2).

Unpaved County Roads (UNPVD). This variable resulted in some striking results from the factor analysis. All but three relationships are significant at the 1% significance level, and these exceptions approach that level. The two relationships in the highest decile group, (5,1) and (6,5), are both income related. The first is a negative correlation and is discussed above under MDFMY; the second, Y < $8K, is positive with almost perfect correlation. Like the former, it is plausible that residents in high-poverty areas cannot command public goods such as hard-surfaced roads. The next level discussed above, (5,2), suggests, and logically follows, that the more out-county work-trip commuters in an area, the fewer the unpaved roads. The next decile contains one correlation, (8,5). As expected, the more urban an area, the lower the incidence of unpaved roads. The lowest decile contains three correlations: (5,3) and (5,4), discussed above, and (7,5), which illustrates a positive relationship between small communities and unpaved roads. This finding surely is not surprising.

Families under $8,000 Annual Income (Y < $8K). All of the coefficients but one discussed above, (6,3), reveal correlations that meet the 1% significance level. The correlations fall into five deciles. The highest, (6,1), almost perfect negatively, was discussed above. The next two decile levels, (6,4) and (6,5), also were discussed above. The fourth decile level contains two negative and significant correlations at the 1% level, (6,2) and (7,6), which were discussed above, and (8,6), Y < $8K:RUK fall into the same category of work-trip commuters traversing county lines. As would be expected, work-trip commuting generally would be constrained by poverty-level income. This fourth level decile contains a positive correlation, %U < 5K:RUK (7,8), which suggests a significant amount of small suburban/ exurban-area inhabitants transitory to out-county urban areas, as would be expected. Further detailed investigation, however, is needed to validate this assumption. The lowest decile contains one negative correlation, (6,3), where the coefficient is significant at the 5% level and has been discussed above.

Incorporated Places Housing under 5,000 Inhabitants (%U < 5K). This variable contains two of the four relationships that do not meet the significance test at the 5% level: (7,2) and (7,3). All the other relationships but one, RUK:%U < 5K (8,7), have been discussed; this particular relationship obtains the highest value among this variable's interactions, although it is negative. This finding suggests that workers from smaller communities commute out-county to urban areas for work.

Rural/Urban Work Commuter Counties Designation (RUK). As discussed above, all the correlations are significant at the 5% level. The positive relationships with the first three variables suggest that a high incidence of rural commuters travel out-county to work activity for higher income levels. The negative relationships suggest that immobile, poverty-level inhabitants in small communities — or along unpaved roads — cannot, do not, or will not commute across county lines to work activity.

Factor Loadings

A further review of the loadings on the sorted factor pattern for each variable reveals an interesting pattern. The values for each variable are as follows, in descending order of variance, explained by this extracted factor pattern:

Variable Number	Variable Descriptor	Factor I Pattern
6	Y < $8K	+ 0.976
1	MDFMY	− 0.972
5	UNPVD	+ 0.890
4	CRLES	+ 0.755
7	%U < 5K	+ 0.700
8	RUK	− 0.680
2	CMUTRS	− 0.621
3	LFPR	− 0.568

These loadings represent the extent to which the variables are related to the hypothetical factors. They suggest an extremely strong relationship between personal income and mobility. Although to a lesser degree, a strong relationship ties rurality to mobility. A moderate relationship also links

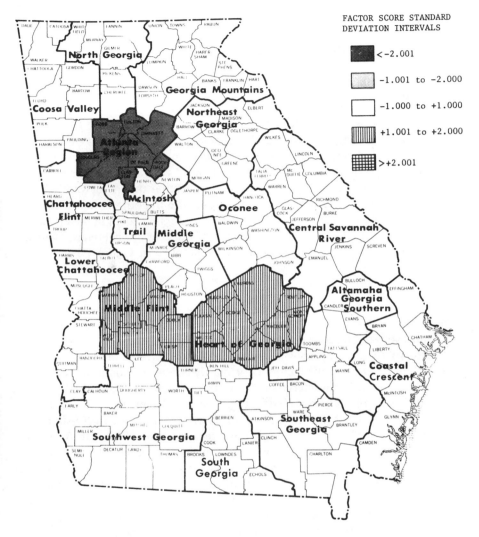

Figure 4.1 Estimated Factor Scores for a Single-Factor Construct Deriving from Eight Variables Interrelating Mobility, Personal Income, and Work Activity for the Area Planning and Development Commissions in Rural Georgia: 1970–1976.

97

work activity to mobility. As mentioned above, the 61.5% of the variance proportion in the variables that overlap with the factor is explained by the communalities obtained after six iterations.

Summary

The results of the APDC factor analysis suggest that the mobility/personal income/work activity model is valid. An extremely large number of the correlations are significant, and the hypothesis is supported by the extraction of a single pattern into a rural mobility/income/work factor. Over 61% of the variance is also explained. Thus it is believed that the factor analysis on the APDCs has provided evidence to support the hypothesis that a cause-and-effect relationship exists among the parameters set forth in the opening chapter of this research. To illustrate some of the geopolitical relationships, the factor scores of the APDC analysis are mapped in Figure 4.1.

FINDINGS: COUNTIES

The factor analysis using the eight variables was performed for all 159 counties and extracted three factor patterns. The factor patterns loaded heavily on factors I and II and somewhat weakly on factor III. Factors I and II both are mobility related, while factor III primarily contains a commuter characterization. Factor I characterizes an income/mobility factor, while factor II characterizes a rurality/mobility factor. The coefficients in the correlation matrix are significant at the 5% level in all but seven of the thirty-six relationships observed. For the Georgia counties, any $r > .159$ is significant at the 0.05 level; any $r > .208$ is significant at the 0.01 level.

Over 67% of the total variance cumulative proportion in the variables that overlap with these factors is explained by the communalities obtained from them after eight iterations. The factor scores, tabularly, indicate no particular pattern or special case. To better illustrate the findings, each score from the factor pattern will be charted on a state base map to exhibit spatial patterns.

Correlation Matrix

The coefficients in the correlation matrix construct shown in Table 4.2 also reveal some interesting relationships. For expediency, the findings in the matrix values are grouped in deciles and discussed in descending order.

Table 4.2 Correlation Coefficients of the Eight-Variable Factor Analysis on the 159 Counties in Georgia

Variable	Factor Correlations							
	1	2	3	4	5	6	7	8
1. MDFMY	1.000							
2. CMUTRS	+.174	1.000						
3. LFPR	+.176	−.185	1.000					
4. CRLES	−.688	−.021	−.147	1.000				
5. UNPVD	−.651	−.060	−.088	+.512	1.000			
6. Y<$8K	−.971	−.155	−.183	+.685	+.625	1.000		
7. %U<5K	−.475	+.285	−.062	+.459	+.449	+.435	1.000	
8. RUK	+.500	−.169	−.013	−.475	−.599	−.463	−.561	1.000

Source: University of Georgia, Geography Department (1979).

Median Family Income (MDFMY). In all cases the relationships are significant at the 5% level. Only correlations CMUTRS:MDFMY (2,1) and LFPR:MDFMY (3,1) are not significant at the 1% level. As expected, the highest decile group reveals that poverty and income are almost perfectly correlated negatively, Y<$8K:MDFMY (6,1). The next decile group contains two strong negative relationships, CRLES:MDFMY (4,1) and UNPVD:MDFMY (5,1). Like the explanation assigned to these same relationships in the APDC analysis, poor households experience more carless conditions than do middle-income households, and poor counties typically contain poor infrastructural facilities. The next decile contains the RUK:MDFMY (8,1) relationship. The higher the income, the more urban the county. The next decile contains the %U<5K:MDFMY (7,1) relationship, which negatively correlated small communities to income. This finding, too, is not surprising. The next and lowest decile finds only two relationships that are not significant at the 1% level; the coefficients are extremely low, and it is difficult for me to ascertain why.

Out-County Work Commuters (CMUTRS). The coefficients for the correlations between this variable and the others reveal some extremely poor relationships, even though three of the values are significant. The highest correlation occurs between %U<5K and CMUTRS, (7,2), which is to be expected, as small-community inhabitants travel out-county to obtain work activity. The next decile group contained LFPR:CMUTRS (3,2), MDFMY: CMUTRS (1,2), RUK:CMUTRS (8,2), and Y<$8K:CMUTRS (6,2). Although out-county work-trip commuting in fact explicates work activity, there apparently is a low relationship in Georgia's counties. This finding stymies any explanation of why this situation exists. The relationship between rural/urban commuting and out-county work-trip commuting was expected to have a high correlation, but the results indicate an extremely low relationship. Similarly, it was expected that a strong *negative* relationship would exist between poverty families and commutation to work activities. To the contrary, however, the correlation, while negative, is low. The remaining decile contains insignificant relationships.

Work Activity (LFPR).   Of this variable, only three of the seven relationships are significant. Two of these, (3,1) and (3,2), have been discussed above. The remaining significant relationship Y < $8K:LFPR (6,3) has, as expected, a negative relationship, but also an unexpectedly low correlation. Poor families are poor quite often simply because they are not participating in work activity. This variable in relation to the other selected variables has not produced the results I had anticipated. This unfulfilled expectation suggests that additional variables, such as unemployment rates and educational attainment levels, should be included in the variable set and explored more thoroughly (see Table 1.6).

Unemployment and educational attainment were considered in the early stages of this research, but were eliminated for different reasons. The former variable was delimited because of its distortion of the nonworker variable. For the educational attainment variable, several attempts to obtain values for the APDC levels were thwarted by the unavailability of data from apparent sources. Contacts were made with the Georgia Data Center (1978), Education Office of Research and Development (1978), and the National Center for Educational Statistics (1978).

Automobile Unavailability (CRLES).   All but two of the relationships to this variable (nonsignificant) attain relatively high correlations. Two fall in the highest decile group: CRLES:MDFMY (4,1), previously discussed, and Y < $8K:CRLES (6,4). This relationship is negative, as expected; it is not unreasonable to assume that a high incidence of carlessness occurs among poverty households. The next decile level contains only one correlation, UNPVD:CRLES (5,4). The same assumption holds for the counties analysis as for the APDCs: a high incidence of carlessness among poverty households would not be uncommon in poor counties experiencing a high incidence of unpaved roads. The next decile level contains two relationships: one positive, %U < 5K:CRLES (7,4), and the other negative, RUK:CRLES (8,4). Like the explanation in the APDC analysis for this same relationship, people in small communities may experience a high incidence of carlessness because work activity is within walking distance of their residence. This explanation is highly unlikely, however. As noted above, carless households in small communities do without because of insufficient economic resources to obtain automobiles. The negative correlation between rural/urban work-trip commuting and carlessness indicates that more carless households are situated in rural counties where surplus work activity is absent than are located in urban counties where excess work activity generally exists.

Unpaved County Roads (UNPVD).   This variable, too, has two insignificant relationships, (5,2) and (5,3), which have already been discussed. Of two others at the highest-decile-group level, one, (5,1), was treated earlier; the other, Y < $8K:UNPVD (6,5), explainable by the constraint of low budget levels in poor counties, which inhibits facilities construction, is a function of poverty conditions. The next decile includes (5,4), which has the same results of (4,5) discussed above, and UNPVD:RUK (5,8). The latter correlation was negative and resulted as expected: the more urban the county, the lower the incidence of unpaved roads. The next decile group contained only one correlation, UNPVD:%U < 5K (5,7). This relationship was positive and resulted as expected: counties with small communities experience a high incidence of unpaved roads. The remaining two interrelationships, (5,2) and (5,3), are not significant.

Families under $8,000 Annual Income (Y < $8K).   All but one relationship, Y < $8K:CMUTRS (6,2), are significant at the 5% level. Only one other, Y < $8K:LFPR (6,3), is not significant at the 1% level. Both were discussed above in their relevant subsections, as were three others, (6,1), (6,4), and (6,5). The remaining two relationships both fall into the same decile group. The first, %U < 5K:Y < $8K (7,6), suggests a moderate positive relationship between poverty and small communities. While some small communities obtain nonpoverty levels primarily, a more detailed review of small communities in rural Georgia revealed a high incidence of low income (*Current Population Report*, 1977). The second, RUK:Y < $8K (8,6), resulted in a moderate negative relationship that suggests workers commuting to urban counties from rural areas would be constrained by poverty-level income.

Incorporated Places Housing under 5,000 Inhabitants (%U < 5K).   This variable contains all relationships but one, %U < 5K:LFPR (7,3), that are significant at the 1% level. The exception, discussed above, is not significant at the 5% level either. All but RUK:%U < 5K (8,7) have been discussed previously. This interrelationship is moderate but negative and, like the APDC result, obtains the highest value among this variable's interactions. Likewise, it suggests that workers who live in smaller communities commute out-county to urban areas for work activity.

Rural/Urban Work Commuter Counties Designation (RUK). All but one of the coefficients, (8,3), are significant at the 5% level; only one other, RUK:CMUTRS (8,2), is not significant at the 1% level. These exceptions, as well as all other relationships, have been discussed above. All the 1% significance relationships but (8,2) are moderate; all but one, RUK: MDFMY (8,1), are negative. This positive exception suggests that a moderate incidence of rural county inhabitants travel out-county to urban work activity for higher-income levels. The four moderate, negative relationships, much like the interpretation for the APDCs, suggest that immobile poverty-level inhabitants from small communities in rural counties or along unpaved roads cannot, do not, or will not commute across county lines to work activity.

Factor Loadings

A detailed review of the loadings on the factor patterns suggest, as hypothesized, that strong relationships do exist among mobility, income, and work conditions in rural Georgia. As noted above, the extracted, rotated factors loaded into three patterns. The values for each variable in each factor, as well as the values for the percent of variance proportions explained by the communalities, are as follows:

Variable Number	Variable Descriptor	Rotated Factor Patterns		
		I	II	III
1	MDFMY	−0.895	+0.416	+0.066
2	CMUTRS	−0.215	−0.198	+0.956
3	LFPR	−0.238	−0.055	−0.258
4	CRLES	+0.567	−0.447	+0.014
5	UNPVD	+0.437	−0.611	−0.091
6	Y < $8K	+0.914	−0.363	−0.031
7	%U < 5K	+0.255	−0.611	+0.229
8	RUK	−0.166	+0.853	−0.037
Percent of Variance Explained		29.0	+25.0	+13.0	=
Total Variance Explained	67.0%			

Factor I. Factor I has been labeled an income/mobility factor. It is quite evident by the extreme heavy loadings on MDFMY and Y < $8K that personal income is very important in the results. While not as strong, two mobility measures, CRLES and UNPVD, experienced moderate loadings. Thus, by the combined strength of these two elements, the income/mobility factor has been extracted from the analysis.

Factor II. Factor II has been labeled a rural/mobility factor. The loadings are heaviest, first, on RUK, the rural/urban designation that delimits geographic distance in commuter/noncommuter counties. Second, the loadings are strong and equal on %U < 5K, small communities, and UNPVD, unpaved county roads. Third, loadings are moderate on CRLES, rural household automobile unavailability, and MDFMY, personal income. By the combined strength of these five elements, the rural/mobility factor has been extracted from the analysis.

Factor III. Factor III has been labeled a commuter/employment factor. A brief look at the loading on CMUTRS, out-county work commuters, reveals the evidence supporting my rationale for applying the label to this factor extraction.

The loadings represent the extent to which the variables selected for this analysis are related to the hypothetical factors. They suggest a strong relationship between mobility, personal income, poverty, rurality, commutation, and employment. Surprisingly, the loadings are not evidenced on work activity as measured by LFPR. This hypothetical inconsistency regarding labor force participation will have to be explored more deeply in future research.

Summary

The results of the Georgia county factor analysis suggest a strong inter-relationship among mobility, personal income, poverty, rurality, and commuter employment. The analysis supports the hypothesis that a relationship exists among the variables, and subsequently the parameters, selected for this research. Three factor patterns were extracted from the analysis, and 67% of the variance is explained. It is believed, therefore, that the factor analysis on Georgia's counties has provided evidence to support the hypothesis that a relationship does exist, in theory if not in fact, among the parameters set forth in the opening chapter of this research.

To illustrate some of the geopolitical relationships, the county factor scores of the analysis are mapped for each of the factor extractions (see Figures 4.2, 4.3, and 4.4).

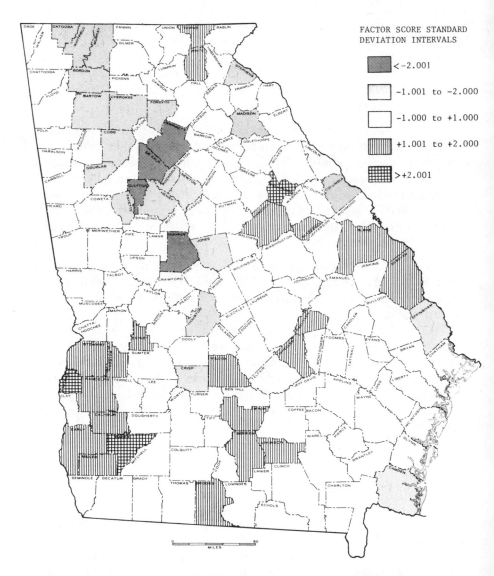

Figure 4.2. Estimated Factor Scores for Extracted Factor Pattern Loadings on Factor I.

104

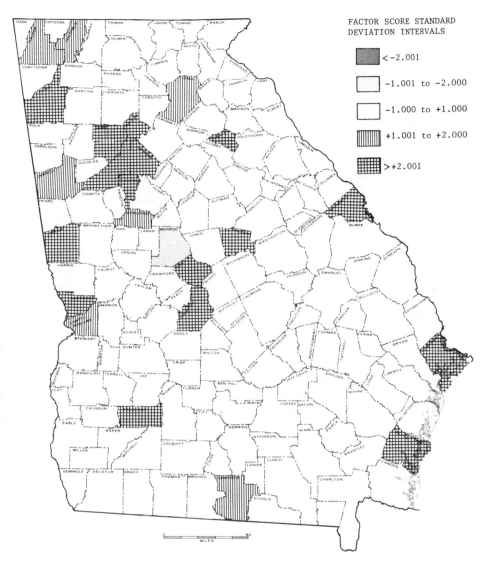

Figure 4.3. Estimated Factor Scores for Extracted Factor Pattern Loadings on Factor II.

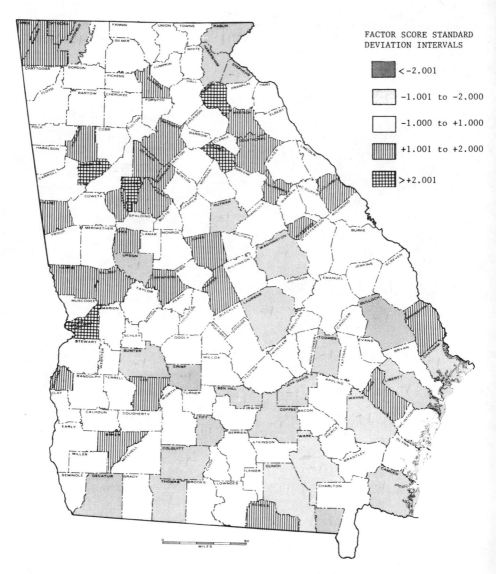

Figure 4.4. Estimated Factor Scores for Extracted Factor Pattern Loadings on Factor III.

SAMPLE CASES

To better illustrate some of the mobility/work activity problems in rural Georgia, an analysis was made of two sample counties. The initial criterion set, a geographical consideration, held that one county would be in the mountains and the other on the coastal plain. The next criterion set, a geopolitical consideration, held that each county would be rural, with no incorporated places housing over 5,000 inhabitants, and would be situated in the APDC containing the largest number of counties. The subsequent criterion set stated that the APDC factor score would fall within the first standard deviation. The results are as follows:

Area	APDC	Factor Score	Number of Counties
Mountains	Georgia Mountains	−0.143	13
Plains	Southwest Georgia	+0.804	14

The counties were then selected from the APDCs. First, all twenty-two counties designated "urban" were deleted. Second, all thirty-nine counties containing incorporated places with more than 5,000 residents were delineated. From the remaining ninety-eight rural counties (eleven in the Georgia Mountains and six in Southwest Georgia), Dawson and Baker, respectively, were chosen irrespective of county factor scores. Other considerations were evaluated and are displayed in Chapter 5 (see Tables 5.1, 5.2, 5.3, and 5.4).

The factor scores for the selected counties are as follows:

| Counties | Factors | | |
	I	II	III
Dawson	+0.886	−0.353	+1.014
Baker	+2.193	−0.028	+1.179

The sample counties analysis is presented in Chapter 5.

5 ANALYSIS OF MOBILITY DISADVANTAGES AND ECONOMIC DEFICIENCIES IN RURAL GEORGIA

Georgia's socioeconomic conditions provide an excellent base for analyzing the geopolitical situation. While the statistics available for each of the variables selected for this research do not describe in detail every person, family, or household, they do provide a level of values that (a) formulates a profile of each area studied and (b) establishes a set of indicators strengthening the hypothesis set forth in the early stages of this study. The data, however, required some modification that minimized skewing distributions and thereby ultimately furthered validation of the model. Originally I believed that aggregation of data to the APDC level alone would be adequate to analyze clearly the mobility disadvantages as they relate to work activity disparities on an areawide basis. This assumption proved to be invalid, however. One approach, which originally included urban indicators, distorted the analysis when the variables describing Georgia were researched either from a holistic perspective or disaggregated into a set of areawide districts. Additionally, the dissimilarity in composition and size of the areawide organizations created some concern regarding the use of the APDCs as the sole geopolitical unit to be studied. The number of counties comprising the eighteen APDCs ranges from five to fourteen. While the size of all the counties is not uniform with respect to square area — that is, inhabitant incidence, roads, places, or densities, among other variables — the use of counties provides a larger universe from which to sample a rural county. As a creature of Public Law 1066, the APDCs can change in terms of county composition merely by a vote on the part of members to exclude themselves from the commission.

For example, the Atlanta area presented some problems. Under Georgia's Public Law 1066, the Atlanta Regional Commission includes seven counties. Under the U.S. Census Bureau definition, the Atlanta Standard Metropolitan Statistical Area increased from five to fifteen counties, some quite rural, between 1972 and 1977. The added counties extend beyond the boundaries of several surrounding APDCs. This research adheres to the seven-county region as designated by the existing commission. Thus it is felt that although the data had been aggregated to APDC levels, results from sampling conditions by county would be more indicative of the mobility disadvantaged in Georgia's rural areas.

Regarding these problems, use of APDC aggregate values overrode the extreme cases of immobility, nonworkers, and low income. Also, in cases where an urban county was situated in an APDC, large populations tended to subsume what were the nonurban residuals of the APDC, thereby masking unfavorable economic conditions in these areas.

Additionally, the use of APDC statistics implies that access to all activities within a given APDC can be obtained with relative ease for a similar effort, provided variations are allowed for distance. This assumption is not valid. While the APDCs do contain a high degree of geographic homogeneity, certain physical barriers exist in the broad expanses of these districts. To be sure, like conditions within a county can be encountered; but the political boundaries often are laid illogically along these physical barriers, thus impeding facilitating improvements. The next section documents some procedures used to eliminate urban bias in the analysis.

PROCEDURES

The factor analysis performed to validate the three-parameter mobility model developed in the hypothesis (see Chapter 1) did so beyond expectations. The results were documented in Chapter 4. In order to attenuate the problem of urban/rural overlap into a wholly rural context, all urban counties were deleted as the first step. The definition of "urban" counties supplied by Dr. Ira Kaye (1977) was used for this delimitation. Following this delimitation, the remaining counties containing places, towns, or cities housing 5,000 or more residents were deleted. Chattahoochee County, an anomaly, fits the definitions for both deleted groups. From the remaining rural counties, a single county was selected as a sample for investigation from each of the two federally designated planning and development regions: the Appalachian Regional Commission and the Coastal Plains Regional Commission. The former contains 35 Georgia counties, and the latter the remaining 124. For purposes of this research, the Plains county was selected from those designated under the original Title V definition of the commission that contained only 89 Georgia counties located geophysically on the continental coastal plain.

RESULTS

Initially, twenty-two counties designated "urban" were deleted. They are detailed as follows (asterisk denotes SMSA central counties):

Baldwin	Fulton*
Bibb*	Glynn
Carroll	Hall
Chatham*	Houston
Chattahoochee	Lowndes
Clarke	Muscogee*
Clayton	Richmond*
Cobb	Spalding
DeKalb	Troup
Dougherty*	Walker
Floyd	Whitfield

The remaining counties designated "nonurban" numbered 137. Of this number, forty-one designated counties containing agglomerations (over 5,000 inhabitants) were deleted. These included the following:

Barrow	Colquitt
Bartow	Coweta
Berrien	Crisp
Bulloch	Decatur
Burke	Douglas
Cattoosa	Early
Chattahoochee	Elbert
Chattooga	Emanuel
Coffee	Gordon

Grady	Sumter
Greene	Terrell
Gwinnett	Thomas
Liberty	Tift
McDuffie	Toombs
Newton	Upson
Peach	Walton
Pike	Ware
Polk	Washington
Rockdale	Wayne
Stephens	Worth

The remaining nonurban counties containing no incorporated places that housed 5,000 or more residents numbered ninety-eight. From this number, Dawson County, located in the Georgia Mountains APDC, was selected to represent a typical mountain area, and Baker County, located in the Southwest Georgia APDC, was the plains area counterpart. The values of the key measures in this research, when compared to the values for the state, provide an indication of the economic disadvantages experienced by the typical household in the selected counties (see Table 5.1).

It is quite evident that a great disparity in income level exists between the inhabitants of the selected counties and the entire state. The typical family in Dawson County receives only little more than half the income of all Georgians, while their counterpart in Baker County receives less than half the state level. The labor force participation in these counties is significantly

Table 5.1.   Median Family Income, Labor Force Participation, and Household Unavailability of Automobiles in Georgia and Selected Sample Counties: 1970–1976

Area	Median Family Income, 1976	Labor Force Participation Rate, 1975	Household Unavailability of Automobiles, 1970
United States	$13,781	61.8%	11.7%
Georgia	12,363	61.5	14.1
Dawson County	7,608	50.0	16.8
Baker County	5,344	51.1	18.7

Source: "The Survey of Buying Power Data Service 1977" (1978); Georgia Department of Labor, Division of Research and Statistics (1977b); and U.S. Department of Commerce, Bureau of Census (1973c, Table 62, pp. 12-100, 12-224–263).

Table 5.2.   Percent of Worker Out-County Commutation, Unpaved County Road Mileage, and Families Receiving Less Than Poverty Level Income in Georgia and Sample Counties: 1970–1976

Area	Workers Out-Commuting, 1970	Unpaved County Road Mileage, 1976	Families Receiving Less than $8,000, 1976
United States	19.2%	22.6%	27.7%
Georgia	26.8	57.0	31.8
Dawson County	45.3	75.7	53.1
Baker County	41.8	71.6	67.5

Source: U.S. Department of Commerce, Bureau of Census (1978b); U.S. Department of Transportation, Planning Data Services Section (1977c); and "The Survey of Buying Power Data Service 1977" (1978).

less than throughout Georgia, by over 10% for each. This difference indicates that fewer job opportunities prevail in these counties than across the rest of the state. The low income level combined with the lower than average labor force participation rate suggests that jobs are more difficult to obtain in these counties than elsewhere in Georgia.

Other variables observed indicate much the same about these counties. While labor force participation in these counties is less than around the state, workers commute to jobs across county lines in substantially greater numbers than do all Georgians. This relatively large commutation occurs even with lower-quality facilities. Despite this extended movement over poorer roads, a much larger share of families receive annual incomes below the $8,000 poverty level. Table 5.2 illustrates the adverse conditions that prevail in these counties.

The data reported in Table 5.2 suggest that more than half again as many workers journey from the home county to work across county lines over more miles of poor roads to receive a substantially lower gross personal income. Given these conditions, one can conclude that with the continual rise in gasoline prices, low-income rural workers would find it more difficult to purchase private transportation.

Other evidence reviewed suggests that these work commuters have few alternatives to this job travel arrangement. Each of the two counties contains less than 5,000 inhabitants. Each contains only one incorporated town-a town with less than 1,000 inhabitants. Neither county, according to the Georgia Department of Industry and Trade (1978a and 1979), had transportation service in the form of bus lines. In addition, a signal factor emerges

Table 5.3. Number of Inhabitants in Dawson and Baker Counties and Their County Seats: 1975

Area	Inhabitants
Dawson County	4,308
Dawsonville	322
Baker County	3,987
Newton	627

Source: Georgia Department of Industry and Trade (1978a, 1979).

signifying that neither county has rail service. Table 5.3 portrays the demographic profile of the sample counties.

Further evidence suggests that job opportunities are slim for job seekers in these counties. Dawson has a total of thirty-two firms with less than 1,300 employed, while Baker has twenty firms with a similar number employed. Data in Table 5.4 illustrate the employment profile of the sample counties.

It is apparent from the data in Table 5.4 that little economic activity adheres to these counties. Approximately as many recruits are available for jobs as are already employed in manufacturing. This fact suggests that the area might support similar-sized activities. Two salient points must be made

Table 5.4. Number of Employees Working in All Firms and Manufacturing and Recruitable Labor in Dawson and Baker Counties (Undated)

	Counties	
	Dawson	Baker
Number Employed		
Total	1,246	1,274
Manufacturing	302	170
Recruitable Labor		
Total	266	193
Experienced	246	180
All Firms/Industries		
Total	32	20
Manufacturing	3	2

Source: Georgia, Department of Industry and Trade (1978a, 1979).

here. First, the manufacturing firms situated in these towns (county seats) are agribusiness and apparel operations, which typically are low paying. Second, no information is given about whether the recruitable labor is employed or nonemployed. (No methodology is provided to determine the agency's derivation.)

Although the information available does not reveal the employment dispersion throughout the county, it is safe to assume that the majority of job opportunities prevails in the county seats of Dawsonville and Newton. It is evident that the manufacturing employment is in these urban places. Clearly, however, the small number of urban inhabitants cannot supply enough workers for all the available jobs in the counties even if every man, woman, and child were employed. We can conclude, therefore, that some workers must travel some mean distances beyond the town limits to work.

Currently no model exists for determining where work activities are distributed geographically in rural areas. Mail surveys were found, in a Georgia Department of Transportation (GDOT) study, to be cumbersome and inefficient (Maggied, 1979, fn. p. 198), while windshield surveys are an expensive method. Similarly, no convenient model is available for identifying where workers reside in relation to their jobs. An origin/destination study performed by road checks would provide this information but is far beyond the scope of this research. Experiences in mail surveys resulted in sparse responses. Field reconnaissance, likewise, is difficult as well as expensive.

Exploration of GDOT county highway maps (1977) reveals little. First of all, no residence symbols appear on the map, rural or urban. (None is designated in the legend.) Second, no structure is drawn to any scale that would indicate the size of operation or incidence of workers. What is revealed by the map symbols, however, is that activities are widely dispersed along the high type paved roads, with few activities on the lower type and unpaved roads. Therefore, no alternative remained to analyze time, distance, and costs other than by setting off activity linkages arbitrarily. This analysis was aided by data extracted from the *Nationwide Personal Transportation Study*, Report No. 8, 1973.

HOME-TO-WORK TRIPS AND TRAVEL

Worker Residence

Thirty percent of the nation's workers reside in incorporated places housing under 5,000 inhabitants. Of the 30% who reside in unincorporated areas, over 44% work at places in unincorporated areas. Likewise, almost 41% of

Table 5.5. Percent of Workers by Selected Place of Residence and Place of Employment in the United States: 1970

| | | Place-of-Employment Areas | | |
Place of Residence	Distribution of Workers	Unincor- porated	Incor- porated	Unknown
Unincorporated Areas	30.0%	44.3%	55.4%	0.3%
Incorporated Places under 5,000	10.0	40.9	57.9	1.2
All Areas and Places	100.0	26.4	73.6	0.0

Source: Svercl and Asin (1973, Table 1, p. 13).

inhabitants residing in incorporated places housing under 5,000 inhabitants work at places in unincorporated areas. Table 5.5 displays the findings more definitively. Svercl and Asin conclude that workers choose similar-sized environments for job and work.

Trip Length

Svercl and Asin also found that almost 42% of the residents in unincorporated areas travel five miles or less in their home-to-work trip, while over 21% travel between six and ten miles to the job. In incorporated places housing under 5,000 inhabitants, over 56% of the residents travel five miles or less, while little more than 12% travel between six and ten miles to the job. Table 5.6 portrays their findings.

Table 5.6. Percent of Workers by Home-to-Work Trip Length and Place of Residence in the United States: 1970

| | Place of Residence | | | |
Home-to-Work Trip Length (Miles)	Unincorporated Areas	Incorporated Places under 5,000	All Places	All Workers
5 or Less	41.8%	56.2%	56.5%	52.1%
6–10	21.1	12.2	20.6	20.9
11–14	8.5	6.5	7.1	7.5
15–19	9.7	8.5	6.8	7.7
20–24	6.8	6.4	3.5	4.5
25–29	11.3	9.8	5.1	6.9
Not Reported	0.8	0.4	0.4	0.4
Total	100.0	100.0	100.0	100.0

Source: Svercl and Asin (1973, Table 2, p. 15).

Table 5.7. Home-to-Work Commuting Time by Selected Place of Residence in the United States: 1970

Place of Residence	Commuting Time (Minutes)					Average All Workers
	15 or Less	16–25	26–35	36 or More	Total	
Unincorporated Areas	50.9	19.1	13.3	16.7	100.0	23
Incorporated Places under 5,000	60.3	16.8	12.9	10.0	100.0	18
All Places and Areas	52.5	19.1	14.0	14.4	100.0	22

Source: Svercl and Asin (1973, Table 3, p. 17).

It is interesting to note, however, that almost 28% of the workers in unincorporated areas and almost 25% in incorporated places housing under 5,000 inhabitants travel fifteen or more miles to work, compared to slightly more than 15% of workers from all places nationwide traveling similar distances. The data also reveal that a smaller portion of the nationwide complement of workers travels these same distances (19%) than of their counterparts in rural and unincorporated areas.

Commuting Time

While average travel varied little, a greater share of inhabitants residing in incorporated places housing under 5,000 spent less time commuting than those inhabitants residing in unincorporated places or in all areas and places. A slightly larger share of commuters in unincorporated areas travel longer time periods than do commuters nationwide. Table 5.7 illustrates these findings more succinctly.

The researchers discovered another interesting finding in their exploration of workers distributed among all income groups: average commuting time per work trip of twenty-two minutes varied little. The eight interval groups examined resulted in a range of nineteen to twenty-five minutes per work trip. Only the group earning over $15,000 annually traveled a significantly longer time period to work. Table 5.8 evidences that outcome. These

Table 5.8   Home-to-Work Commuting Time by Household Income in the United States: 1970

Annual Household Income*	Average Commuting Time (Minutes)
$ 2,999 and Under	20
3,000–3,999	19
4,000–4,999	22
5,000–5,999	23
6,000–7,499	20
7,500–9,999	21
10,000–14,999	22
15,000 and Over	25
All Income Groups	22

Source: Svercl and Asin (1973, Table 4, p. 18).
*It is understood that income levels of a decade ago as such are meaningless in view of the extensive inflation that occurred in the seventies, without application of implicit price deflaters. The evidence distributed over all income groups, however, provides some measure of evaluation for analysis purposes.

Table 5.9. Percent of Home-to-Work Trips and Miles of Travel by Transportation Mode and Selected Place of Residence in the United States: 1970

| Place of Residence | Private Automobile | | | Public | |
	Driver	Passenger	Total	Conveyance	Other
Person Trips					
Unincorporated Areas	65.0%	18.8%	83.8%	2.6%	13.6%
Incorporated Places under 5,000	64.0	18.4	82.4	3.1	14.5
All Areas and Places	64.4	18.3	82.7	8.4	8.9
Person Miles					
Unincorporated Areas	60.0 miles	19.6 miles	79.6 miles	4.3 miles	16.1 miles
Incorporated Places under 5,000	56.4	13.5	69.9*	8.0*	22.1*
All Areas and Places	59.7	18.1	77.8	10.2	12.0

Source: Svercl and Asin (1973, Table 5, p. 23).
Note: Data in source table do not sum to 100%.

findings tend to substantiate Wheeler's (1974) assertion that higher-income families travel longer in commuting to work than do their lower-income counterparts.

Place of Residence

Nationwide, almost 83% of all home-to-work *person trips* for all areas and places were transited by automobile, with only another 10% of the workers using public conveyances. Similarly, almost 78% of the *person miles* were by automobile, with slightly over 10% of the people using public conveyances. Little difference exists in private automobile usage between small and all areas, but public transportation usage shows a significantly different outcome. Table 5.9 provides a view of these differences.

Significantly fewer persons from small places and areas used public conveyances for work trips than did persons nationwide. The person-mile factor presents a different picture, however. While the share of residents from unincorporated areas transit by public conveyance significantly less than the nation as a whole, their counterparts residing in incorporated places with under 5,000 inhabitants do not deviate substantially from the national average. This similarity may be due to a large number of small-sized suburbs that may share some form of common public service with contiguous urban areas. The Svercl and Asin (1973) study does not reveal whether the public conveyance is limited to intracity service or includes interurban transit. While no specific analysis was performed for this research, it was learned that substantial numbers of Georgia's rural residents travel to work daily on the interurban bus.

The companion finding in the Svercl and Asin research suggests that this assumption is valid. Their analysis of transits by place of residence revealed that work-trip length by bus and streetcar was longest in places housing under 5,000 inhabitants and in unincorporated areas. Table 5.10 illustrates the findings.

Although there are no data to support our assumption, the evidence in Table 5.10 suggests that residents in rural areas and small places would benefit from public-funded transit equally if not more than their counterparts in larger urban areas. They travel longer and farther; thus it is safe to assume that the trip is more costly in both time and dollars. For the poor and low-income families addressed in this research, I believe that these costs are the difference between getting to work and not getting to work.

Svercl and Asin (1973) make another interesting paradoxical observation that supports our hypothesis about the burden that the poor must carry in

Table 5.10. Average Home-to-Work Trip Length by Selected
Transits and Place of Residence in the United States: 1970

	Average Trip Length Mileage	
Place of Residence	Automobile	Bus and Streetcar
Unincorporated Areas	11.1	15.4
Incorporated Places under 5,000	7.9	27.7
All Areas and Places	9.4	8.7

Source: Svercl and Asin (1973, Table 16, p. 24).

their journey to work. Both the lowest and the highest income groups make
more than half of their work trips by private vehicle; the cumulative intermediate groups make *less than half* of their work trips by similar transits.
Table 5.11 illustrates the differences.

The implications from the data are not surprising. The data indicate that
as income increases, the choice of journey-to-work transit increases. This
indication holds for the private automobile. It holds in every case for public
transportation, except for the highest income group. This deviation may
occur because of a relatively high incidence of train commuters in this income bracket compared to other brackets. Apparently this phenomenon
occurs because the higher-income recipients consider it more time efficient
to transit by train than to drive.

The interesting finding relates to the share of the employed who walk to

Table 5.11. Percent of Workers in Household Income Group Intervals by
Selected Transits for Home-to-Work Trips in the United States: 1970

Annual Household Income	Private Automobile	Public Conveyance	Combination*	Walking	Other
Under $3,000	45.7%	12.8%	1.5%	11.9%	28.1%
3,000–3,999	48.5	12.5	2.1	12.7	24.2
4,000–4,999	56.1	11.6	1.9	7.0	23.4
5,000–5,999	63.7	9.4	1.3	5.5	20.1
6,000–7,499	67.2	6.9	3.1	5.3	17.5
7,500–9,999	70.3	5.9	2.4	4.5	16.9
10,000–14,999	74.1	5.1	3.3	2.9	14.6
15,000 and over	75.2	6.5	4.5	3.3	10.5
All Employed	67.4	7.2	2.9	5.0	17.4

Source: Svercl and Asin (1973, Table 10, p. 28).
*Refers to split transits of private automobile and public conveyance or other.

work. Not walking appeared to be a function of income. Over 27% of the walkers earned less than $4,000 in 1969. Of those workers earning less than $3,000, almost 12% walked; of those earning between $3,000 and $4,000, almost 13% walked. In the higher-income classes, a substantial drop in the incidence of walkers is observed.

Since the study from which these data are extracted is nationwide, it is safe to assume that most walkers reside and work in urban areas where generally the infrastructure for walking (sidewalks) is in place. In this analysis, disaggregation of the study data between urban and rural was evident.

While little relationship exists between income and travel time, the average time spent commuting from home to work varies substantially among sector modes. Alex (1974) found that time spent in personal transit vehicles is slightly over half the time spent in fixed-route travel. Such "personal transit" includes private automobiles, motorcycles, and demand-responsive service such as taxis and jitneys. A "fixed route," on the other hand, includes services that operate on a public way (road or rail), such as buses, streetcars, subways, and some jitneys. Home-to-work commuting time spent in personal transit averages 20 minutes, with a range from 18 to 22 minutes, while time spent in fixed-route travel averages 38 minutes, with a range of 32 to 49 minutes. Of significant importance, however, is that commuting time for the lowest and highest income brackets is nearly two and one-half times longer by fixed route than by personal transit (see Table 5.12).

Despite the incidence of public conveyance usage as reported in Table 5.11, "more than half of all commuters indicated that public transportation is not available" (Svercl and Asin, 1973, p. 36). Svercl and Asin postulate that distance to public conveyances and services influences a user's options when (or if) transiting to work. While perception and opinion (a subjective matter) play a role in the user's decision, Svercl and Asin set discrete dis-

Table 5.12 Average Home-to-Work Commuting Time by Sector Mode and Selected Annual Household Income Intervals in the United States: 1970

Annual Household Income	Minutes Traveled	
	Personal Transit	Fixed Route
Under $3,000	18	42
Over $15,000	21	49
All Intervals	20	38

Source: Svercl and Asin (1973, Table 16, p. 35).

Table 5.13   Percent of Workers by Selected Place of Residence, Availability of Public Transportation from Home to Work, and Means Used in the United States: 1970

| | Public Transportation | | |
| | Not | | Not |
Place of Residence	Available	Available	Reported
	Users of All Sector Modes		
Unincorporated Areas	71.3%	27.3%	1.4%
Incorporated Places under 5,000	87.5	11.2	1.3
All Areas and Places	51.7	47.2	1.1
	Users of Private Automobiles		
Unincorporated Areas	73.4	25.3	1.3
Incorporated Places under 5,000	89.3	9.3	1.4
All Areas and Places	58.1	40.8	1.1
	Users of Public Conveyance		
Unincorporated Areas	*	95.8	4.2
Incorporated Areas under 5,000	*	100.0	*
All Areas and Places	0.5	98.9	0.6

Source: Svercl and Asin (1973, Table 17, p. 36).
*Data statistically insignificant for analysis.

tance parameters, including "over six blocks" and "no public transit available," which indicate that walking much over a half-mile is beyond the acceptable limits that a commuter is willing to withstand. A brief analysis of the data in Table 5.13 indicates the availability of public transportation to workers.

As expected, users of public conveyances reported nearly unanimously that service is available to them. On the other hand, users of all sectors, as well as users of private automobiles for work commuting who reside in unincorporated areas and particularly in incorporated places housing under 5,000 inhabitants, indicated that public conveyances were unavailable to them. These findings substantially depart from the findings indicated for commuters residing in all areas and places. The findings also support one of the major assumptions underlying this research: *public transportation conveyance is not available* for most rural inhabitants who reside in unincorporated areas or in incorporated places housing under 5,000 inhabitants — an assumption that applies to Georgia.

An important finding in the home-to-work study reveals that while peak hour home-to-work commuting occurs between 6:00 A.M. and 9:00 A.M. and

Table 5.14. Average Home-to-Work Trip Length by
Selected Departure Hour in the United States: 1970

Departure Hour	All Transit Trip Miles	Automobile Trip Miles
4:00 A.M.	19.2	14.0
5:00 A.M.	14.6	14.0
6:00 A.M.	12.7	11.6
7:00 A.M.	9.9	10.0
8:00 A.M.	8.0	8.1
12:00 N	5.9*	5.6*
4:00 P.M.	10.0	10.1
12:00 M	10.0	8.4
All Hours	9.9	9.4

Source: Svercl and Asin (1973, Table A–9, p. 60).
*The shortest average work-trip length start occurs at noon.

between 3:00 P.M. and 6:00 P.M., average trip lengths generally are longest
when begun between 4:00 A.M. and 6:00 A.M. Table 5.14 shows the distance
a typical commuter travels at different times of the morning.

While the early morning hour departures are relatively small, they nonetheless do occur; they occur at times when most of the public transportation, other than in large metropolitan areas, is not scheduled to run. In
small places, public conveyances virtually do not exist before 6:00 A.M. and
generally do not exceed two runs per hour between 6:00 A.M. and 9:00 A.M.
(Bruton, 1977). Reliance on private automobiles approaches 100%. A distribution of trip time departures is shown in Table 5.15.

No data aggregations are available by state or local areas, according to
Svercl and Asin (1973). The indicators presented above were extracted from
a special sample survey performed by the Census Bureau for the Federal
Highway Administration. The 235 sample areas were selected by grouping
all the nation's counties and independent cities into about 1,900 primary
sample units (PSUs) and further forming 235 strata containing one or more
PSUs that are relatively homogeneous according to socioeconomic characteristics. The survey was based on a multistage probability sample of housing units located in 235 sample areas. These areas comprised 485 counties
and independent cities representing every state and the District of Colum-
bia. The purpose of presenting this set of national statistics is to illustrate
where small areas are deficient or hindered by their relative size. The survey
revealed that very lowest income recipients travel farther to work than any
income group other than the very highest in their study; and this behavior

Table 5.15. Percent of Automobile Work Trips and Miles of Travel by Trip Purpose and Selected Departure Hour in the United States: 1970

| | Percent Home to Work of All Trip Purposes | | | |
| | Automobile Trips | | Travel Miles | |
Departure Hour	Daily	Hourly	Daily	Hourly
4:00 A.M.	0.1%	54.8%	0.1%	23.7%
5:00 A.M.	0.7	85.5	1.0	65.0
6:00 A.M.	3.0	87.5	3.8	79.3
7:00 A.M.	5.1	75.5	5.7	72.5
8:00 A.M.	2.9	50.8	2.6	45.4
12:00 N	1.2	21.1	0.8	17.6
4:00 P.M.	3.7	41.0	4.2	41.4
12:00 M	0.4	35.2	0.5	34.6
Total	31.8*	N/A	33.6*	N/A

Source: Svercl and Asin (1973, Table A–27, p. 78).
*Total departures "for all trip purposes" total 100%.

prevails in view of the finding that workers tend to live in a place size of similar magnitude to their workplace size. While no data indicated commuter time departure by place size or occupation, earlier-hour trip departures tended to be longer in duration and distance. The finding suggests to me, intuitively, that these early morning long-distance commuters reside in small rural areas.

Apparently, use of public transportation has not changed significantly even in urban areas. The most recent study on travel to work in twenty-one SMSAs revealed that only 12% used public conveyance (U.S. Department of Commerce, 1978). Eighty-six percent used private automobile or truck (this share includes car pooling). Median distance for all SMSAs equaled 7.5 miles, while Atlanta held the longest median distance at 9.8 miles. (All SMSA commuters using public conveyance traveled a median distance of 8.9 miles.)

Since the automobile is the predominant transit used nationwide for home-to-work commuting, with under 10% occurring on public conveyance, it is difficult to imagine that public conveyance operation in sparsely populated small areas would be technically practicable, given the typical eleven-hour home-to-work workday. It is even more difficult to imagine that such an operation would be economically feasible with some sort of double work-shift change required by drivers. Moreover, it is nearly impossible to believe that such a carriage operation would be politically tenable. A brief analysis of the distances and road conditions of the selected Georgia counties reveals the impossibility of operating viable public transportation service in the urban hinterlands and small places of rural Georgia. A view of the time schedule required to travel between the incorporated places in the two sample counties provides some insights into the reason why public conveyance in rural areas is not technically practicable even on well-maintained roads. Typically, this notion is explicated as travel times between city-pairs; in the rural context, link-node is used in lieu of city-pair.

ANALYSIS OF SAMPLE COUNTIES IN RURAL GEORGIA

Travel Times

Travel time (speed) is a calculated average time period required for a private automobile, under optimum conditions, to travel between two points (nodes) on a specified segment (link) of state-maintained, numbered roadways. In this research I assigned each segment an average speed based on road surface, contour, terrain, width, urbanization, and other factors designated in "The Yellow Book" (Georgia, 1973), mandated by the Federal Highway Administration.

Travel times scheduled on the link-nodes for each sample county numbered six; each county had five intercounty linkages and one intracounty linkage that lay between the single-county incorporated place and another census-county division. The linkages and the travel times schedule are listed in Table 5.16.

In both cases, the minimum travel time along any link-node requires approximately twenty minutes. Newton is situated along the Baker-Mitchell County line contiguous to the Flint River, atypical of most single incorporated nodal places. In both cases, the nearest growth center is over one-half hour's drive; with one exception in each county, out-county commuters require approximately one-half hour driving time. Albany, in Baker County, and Gainesville, in Hall County, are the nearest cities — growth centers — with evident diversified employment opportunities.

A look at the sample county maps reveals some human activities that are widely dispersed throughout the sample counties. No households are charted on the detailed county highway maps. U.S. Geological Survey quadrangle maps do chart them, but revisions often are not made for contiguous areas in the same time period. Thus, discrepancies appear between areas when spliced into a photomosaic, and so they were not explored for this research. Because these activities are so widely dispersed, overall daily

Table 5.16.   Travel Time for Link-Nodes Connecting Incorporated Places in Selected Rural Georgia Counties: 1973

Base County	Base Node	Connected Node	Connected County	Travel Time (Minutes)
Baker	Newton	Milford	Baker	21
	Newton	Bainbridge	Decatur	59
	Newton	Camilla	Mitchell	18
	Newton	Damascus	Early	48
	Newton	Leary	Calhoun	32
	Newton	Albany	Dougherty	43
Dawson	Dawsonville	North Dawsonville CCD*	Dawson	18
	Dawsonville	Silver City	Forsyth	22
	Dawsonville	Gainesville	Hall	36
	Dawsonville	Nelson	Pickens	39
	Dawsonville	Jasper	Pickens	50
	Dawsonville	Dahlonega	Lumpkin	26

Source: Georgia Department of Transportation, Division of Planning and Programming (1978b).

*CCD denotes County-Census Division. The node in this case is at the crossroads in Juno, an unincorporated area. Milford also is a node on a crossroads in an unincorporated area.

travel schedules require substantially more time for commuting to any job center than implied in Table 5.16. Discussions with APDC planning directors and transportation planners indicated that feedback from their clientele revealed that rural work trips, particularly return trips, deviated from their home-to-work "line haul" because of shopping, children's activities, and other attractions that were not on the direct work-trip route. Thus trip schedules may be longer than structured study findings suggest.

Without extensive "origin and destination" studies for each county, moreover, there is no way to ascertain exactly where workers reside in relation to their job sites. Even less opportunity occurs to determine where nonworkers reside. It is, however, conceivable that co-workers do not necessarily live in the same vicinity — particularly in rural areas — and that carless nonworkers who are desirous of jobs do not reside near workers who commute to areas where job opportunities prevail. Without information to substantiate a need, no case can be made to support a program that would provide public conveyances for potential rural work commuters. To compensate for the dearth of data pertaining to residential site dispersion, a hypothetical problem situation was constructed for the two sample counties. Two link-nodes in each county were selected that had a common terminus in the county incorporated place to structure a "transit loop" that would result in triangular routes. These routes contained road segments that were beyond the state numbered network. The routes tied to out-county linkages in another direction to an incorporated place where hypothetical jobs might exist. After being analyzed separately, the travel times and distances for each separate route were summed and applied to a typical work starting time of 8:00 A.M. If additional passengers who are not located on the loop route require portal pickup at their residence, either within the interstice or in its hinterland, it is possible that not enough time would exist to deposit the passengers at their work sites on time. The results of the sample indicate why the added commutation time necessary for a widely dispersed two-stop commuting trip excessively extends a moderate workday.

Baker County. In Baker County, Newton was the home base for the mythical public conveyance with Camilla (population 4,943) to the southeast, as the shortest link-node connecting to the neighboring county. It was assumed that job commuters resided in Milford, over 14 miles distant and 21 minutes northwest, and at Live Oaks, about 13 miles distant and 26 minutes west. Live Oaks and Milford are located about 9 miles distant and 20 minutes apart in the north-south direction. The sketch map in Figure 5.1

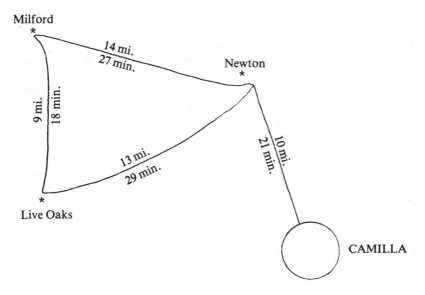

Figure 5.1. Sketch Map for Hypothetical Dispersion of Workers' Residences Using a Single Transit Conveyance to Camilla, Georgia, from Hinterland Hamlets in Baker County.

Table 5.17. Hypothetical Journey-to-Work Commuting Times and Distances for Selected Link-Nodes, Baker County: 1973

Work Commuter Link-Node	Time in Minutes*	Distance in Miles
Newton to Camilla	21	10
Milford to Newton	27	14
Live Oaks to Newton	29	13
Live Oaks to Milford**	18	9

Source: Derived estimates from Georgia Department of Transportation, Division of Planning and Programming (1977c, 1978b).

*Travel times were developed as mean averages calculated from five actual trips driven by Georgia Transportation District personnel in each of Georgia's seven transportation districts under the supervision of the Highway Planning Data Service Office. Trip times were run during morning peak, morning ebb, noonday (lunch) acceleration, evening peak, and evening ebb hours.

**Estimates based on intermittent discussions with Danny Lamb, Senior Planner, Georgia Department of Transportation, January to December 1978.

depicts the area. Table 5.17 displays the Baker County sample journey-to-work commuting times and distances.

The least scheduled time without intervening pickup stops from Milford to Camilla requires 48 minutes (over 28 miles), while the least scheduled time from Live Oaks to Camilla requires 50 minutes (over 27 miles) — substantial rides, indeed. Assuming that work commences at 8:00 A.M., departure should be scheduled by 7:00 A.M. If a single-vehicle trip were to initiate in Newton to call for both commuters, the 50-mile trip would require 95 minutes' travel time. This means the Newton departure would have to occur no later than 6:15 A.M. If no riders are boarded before reaching these outlying towns, at least one passenger must ride an added 18 minutes and 9 miles beyond his or her own single scheduled travel time during this journey to work.

Dawson County. In Dawson County, Dawsonville was the home base for the mythical public conveyance, with Dahlonega to the north (population 2,757) the next shortest link-node connecting to Dawson County. The shortest link-node to Silver City was not used as the job center because Silver City is little more than a crossroads with few inhabitants residing nearby. It is assumed that job commuters reside in Silver City over 6 miles and 22

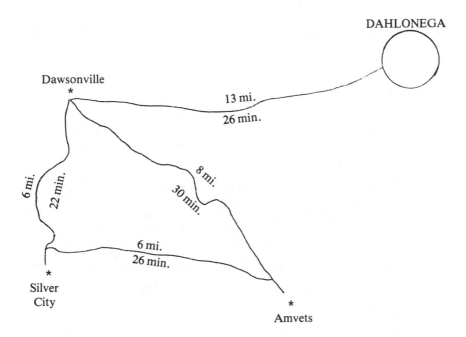

Figure 5.2. Sketch Map for Hypothetical Dispersion of Workers' Residences Using a Single Transit Conveyance to Dahlonega, Georgia, from Hinterland Hamlets in Dawson County.

minutes south and in Amvets almost 8 miles and 30 minutes southeast. Silver City and Amvets are located about 6 miles and 26 minutes apart in an east-west direction. The terrain is quite hilly, and the roadway is correspondingly curvy. The sketch map in Figure 5.2 portrays the general configuration of the area and the selected sample routes. Table 5.18 presents the Dawson County sample journey-to-work commuting times and distances.

The least time required to traverse without pickup stops from Silver City to Dahlonega is 48 minutes over a distance of 19 miles, while the least time required to travel from Amvets to Dahlonega is 59 minutes over a distance of 21 miles. Assuming that work in Dahlonega commences at 8:00 A.M., departure should be scheduled at 7:00 A.M. for the former and 6:45 A.M. for the latter. If a single-vehicle trip were to originate in Dawsonville to call for both commuters, the 33-mile trip would require 104 minutes. This means that the Dawsonville departure would have to occur no later than 6:00 A.M. If no riders are boarded before reaching these outlying towns, at least one passenger must ride an added 26 minutes and 6 very rough miles beyond his or her own single scheduled travel time during the journey to work.

Table 5.18.   Hypothetical Journey-to-Work Commuting
Times and Distances for Selected Link-Nodes, Dawson
County: 1973

Work Commuter Link-Node	Time in Minutes*	Distance in Miles
Dawsonville to Dahlonega	26	13
Silver City to Dawsonville	22	6
Amvets to Dawsonville	30	8
Amvets to Silver City**	26	6

Source: Derived estimates from Georgia Department of Transportation, Division of Planning and Programming (1977d, 1978b).

*Travel times were developed as mean averages calculated from five actual trips driven by Georgia Transportation District personnel in each of Georgia's seven transportation districts under the supervision of the Highway Planning Data Service Office. Trip times were run during morning peak, morning ebb, noonday (lunch) acceleration, evening peak, and evening ebb hours.

**Estimates based on intermittent discussions with Danny Lamb, Senior Planner, Georgia Department of Transportation, January to December 1978.

Travel Costs

Travel costs, which are a function of vehicle-operating costs, have been rising rapidly in recent years. Between 1960 and 1976, ten-year total costs across the nation nearly doubled. Between 1974 and 1976, these decennial costs rose by 12.5% (see Table 5.19).

The data also indicate that following a quinquennium of declining annual operating costs per mile, the cost rises significantly between the fifth and seventh year of operation. This finding suggests that older cars are more costly to operate. The finding relates to the problem cited in the previously referenced assertion by Meyer and Kain (1968, p. 5): poor people own poor cars; thus they must pay a higher per-mile operating cost; thus they bear a larger burden in their expense budget for transportation than do the nonpoor.

Attempts to gather vehicle-operating costs that were more pertinent, more recent, and more localized to rural Georgia proved fruitless. Discussion with officials in the Georgia Transportation Department revealed that the most recent study (1979) providing such information about a "nearby" area similar to Georgia was performed for the state of Arkansas covering the year 1977 and was based on size of automobile. The results of the study

Table 5.19. Estimated Cost of Operating an Automobile in the United States: 1960–1979

January 1, Annual	Ten-Year Total Costs	Ten-Year Average	Cents-per-Mile Cost: Selected Age Year					
			First	Third	Fifth	Seventh	Tenth	
1960	$ 9,761	9.76¢	NR*	NR*	NR*	NR*	NR*	
1970	11,890	11.89	14.21	12.10	11.50	12.02	10.82	
1974	15,892	15.89	16.74	15.91	15.08	17.41	15.79	
1976	17,879	17.88	18.73	17.79	17.04	19.94	17.63	
1979	24,600	24.60	27.20	24.20	27.30	29.20	23.30	
Total Estimated Miles Traveled			14,500	11,500	9,900	9,500	5,700	

Source: U.S. Department of Commerce, Bureau of Census, Statistical Abstract of the United States, Washington, D.C.: U.S. GPO, 1971, 1974, 1976, 1979, Table 854, p. 537 in 1970 Abstract; Table 935, p. 560 in 1974 Abstract; Table 1068, p. 640 in 1977 Abstract; Table 1099, p. 654 in 1980 Abstract.
*NR denotes not reported.

stated that operating costs ranged from 12.6 cents to 17.9 cents per mile. While even the upper limit of the Arkansas range appears low compared to the Hertz Rent-a-Car (1976) estimates, discussed in Chapter 1, of 23 cents per mile during 1974, and equals the ten-year average report by the Census Bureau for 1976 (see Table 5.19), the Arkansas rural/urban ratio comports more to the Georgia condition than either Arkansas or Georgia does to the entire nation. The rural population of Arkansas and Georgia in 1970 approximated 50% and 40%, respectively, while the nation's rural population approached 26%.

Based on the nationwide vehicle-operating costs presented in Table 5.19 and the Arkansas study, it was assumed that 17.9 cents would be valid to apply to the distance factors presented in Tables 5.17 and 5.18 for Baker and Dawson counties, respectively. The "ten-year average" nearly equates to the *Statistical Abstract*'s (U.S. Department of Commerce, 1977b) "third-year" value for 1976 of 17.79 cents and the Arkansas upper limit of 17.9 cents. Since the share of cars and trucks in use "under three years of age" has been falling, and the share "three to five years of age" has been rising, the "third year" value was felt to be a valid multiplier and thus applicable to this research. The two sample work trips for the typical commuter are costed in the analyses below. They are described as end-to-end trips without mention of the sample county intermediate incorporated place. The link-nodes were summed and raised by a factor of two to accommodate the return trip home.

Baker County. The work-trip routes from Baker County were between Milford and Camilla and between Live Oaks and Camilla, both via Newton. Table 5.20 reveals the results of the Baker County Analysis.

Table 5.20. Journey-to-Work Commuter Costs by Privately Owned Automobile for Selected Work-Trip Routes, Baker County: 1976

Work-Trip Routes	Time in Minutes	Distance in Miles	Costs* One Way	Round Trip
Milford to Camilla	48	24	$4.30	$8.59
Live Oaks to Camilla	50	23	4.12	8.23

Source: Time in minutes and distance in miles summed from data in Table 5.18. One-way costs are derived estimates based on a 17.9¢-per-mile expenditure, and round-trip costs are raised by a factor of two.

*Detail may not compute to total due to rounding.

Table 5.21.   Journey-to-Work Commuter Costs by Privately Owned Automobile for Selected Work-Trip Routes, Dawson County: 1976

Work-Trip Routes	Time in Minutes	Distance in Miles	Costs* One Way	Round Trip
Silver City to Dahlonega	48	19	$3.40	$6.80
Amvets to Dahlonega	56	21	3.76	7.52

Source: Time in minutes and distance in miles summed from data in Table 5.19. One-way costs are derived estimates based on a 17.9¢-per-mile expenditure, and round-trip costs are raised by a factor of two.

*Detail may not compute to total due to rounding.

Dawson County.   The work-trip routes in Dawson County were between Silver City and Dahlonega and between Amvets and Dahlonega, both via Dawsonville. Table 5.21 reveals the results of the Dawson County analysis.

Further analysis corroborates the hypothesis stated in the early stages of this research (Chapter 1): rural commuters from the sample counties tested in Georgia for 1976 spent an inordinate share of their gross personal income for work trips. Based on a 260-day work year, the typical worker in Baker and Dawson counties, Georgia, consumed 40.9% and 24.5%, respectively, of their gross personal income for their daily work-trip commuting expenditure. Table 5.22 presents the results of the analysis.

Table 5.22.   Percent of Gross Personal Income Required for Hypothetical Daily Journey-to-Work Trips from Baker and Dawson Counties to Adjacent County Job Centers: 1976

Area	Median Family Income	Daily Gross Income	Average Trip Cost	Percent of Gross Personal Income for Trip
Baker County	$5,344	$20.55*	$8,41**	40.9%
Dawson County	7,608	29.26*	7.16**	24.5

Source: Derived estimates from data in Tables 5.1, 5.20, and 5.21.

*Values based on a 260-day work year.

**Average trip cost is mean average of sample trip cost estimates derived in Tables 5.20 and 5.21.

Table 5.23 Incidence of Deficiencies and Relationships among work Activity, Mobility, and personal Income from Derived FActors for Selected Counties in Rural Georgia: 1970-1976

| County | Percent Nonworkers | Percent Immobility | | Index of Gross Income Deficiency | | Percent Job Deficiency |
		Carless	Roadless	Personal Income	Poverty	
Baker	11.5%	4.6%	14.6%	0.43	35.7%	15.0%
Dawson	10.4	2.7	18.7	0.62	21.3	18.5

Source: Designated with each factor listed in note below.

Note: Nonworkers are the residual of Georgia labor force participation rates minus the sample county rates; data based on Table 5.1.

Immobility is the residual of Georgia household vehicle unavailability rates and unpaved roads minus the sample county rates; data based on Tables 5.1 and 5.2.

Income deficiency values are measured against the aggregate values of the entire state; *personal income* is a link relative index of median family income absolute values compared to the Georgia value of 1.00, while *poverty* is the residual of Georgia families' annual gross income under $8,000 level minus the sample county rates; data based on Tables 5.1 and 5.2.

Job deficiency is the residual of Georgia county out-commuter rates minus the sample county rates; data based on Table 5.2.

SUMMARY AND CONCLUSIONS

When viewing the results of the analysis performed in this research, it is not difficult to ascertain why a deficiency in labor force participation exists for the sample counties. Over 41% (see Table 5.2) of their workers had to commute longer distances beyond the county line during longer periods for work, while at least 17% (see Table 5.1) of the sample counties' other inhabitants had no automobiles available to them. When an assumption was made that little or no car pooling occurred in these sample counties, below-poverty-level and inordinately low incomes further exacerbated the problem, such that substantially more than half the families fell into that costly, interminably long commutation class (see Table 5.2). This evidence, coupled with the findings revealed in the trip cost analysis, leads to the conclusion that high work-trip transit costs lead to a substantial share of nonworkers in these rural hinterlands. A recapitulation of the above information in tabular form will more readily express the relationships among the parameters in the problem statement (see Chapter 1). Table 5.23 presents a profile of these relationships.

Given the findings in Table 5.23, the conditions in these sample counties look bleak indeed. Programs and procedures intended to correct some deficiencies reported above have been enacted (see Chapter 3), while fewer have been promulgated as demonstration packages; but the immobility factor related to rural work commuting, rural job activity, and rural personal income has been obfuscated by inclusion into transportation projects that are designed to assist the elderly and the handicapped. To be sure, elderly and handicapped programs are sorely needed, but elderly and handicapped clientele generally — with exceptions — can be served between 8:00 A.M. and 5:00 P.M. Throughout the literature search, special cases unique to specific geographic areas, particular clientele problems, and strident administration constraints were discovered. It is not within the scope of this research to discuss them.

In order not to belabor the obvious, suffice it to say that elderly and handicapped programs *do not fit the needs of the nonworker* who may be the potential hinterland commuter if the economic conditions in his or her rural habitat were changed by more effective job transits. The analyses performed in this chapter for the sample counties in rural Georgia only begin to address the myriad problems associated with rural transportation. It is, however, an important step for public administrators and policy planners to realize that the mobility/personal income/work activity relationship does in fact exist. Chapter 6 will recommend some programs that may be technically practicable.

6 CONCLUSIONS AND RECOMMENDATIONS ON MOBILITY DISADVANTAGES IN RURAL REACHES

This chapter lists the major conclusions indicated from the findings in the literature search and task analyses undertaken in the previous chapters. It states recommendations that should help public administrators and policy planners to identify the problem areas, formulate alternative solutions, and resolve the issues by (1) promulgating relevant existing programs, (2) innovating practicable new programs, and (3) combining the two into feasible programs that contain an acceptable and reasonable probability of success.

CONCLUSIONS

- A strong relationship exists between mobility, personal income, and work activity.
- Rural workers commute longer distances to work than do their urban counterparts.
- Rural workers travel longer time periods to work than do their urban counterparts.
- Rural commuters in Georgia spend more money for work trips than do their urban counterparts.

- Rural commuters in Georgia hinterlands spend an inordinate, regressive share of their personal time and income for journey-to-work transits.
- Job opportunities are farther away from home for rural inhabitants than for their urban counterparts.
- Job opportunities are fewer in residence counties for Georgia's rural inhabitants than for their urban counterparts.
- Nonworker incidence is greater in Georgia's rural counties than in their urban counterparts.
- Personal income levels are lower for Georgia's rural families than for their urban counterparts.
- Poverty levels are higher for Georgia's rural families than for their urban counterparts.
- Immobility incidence is greater in Georgia's rural counties than in their urban counterparts.
- Alternative transits for personal transportation in Georgia's rural counties seldom, if ever, exist.
- Communication facilities incidence is lower in Georgia's rural counties than in their urban counterparts.
- Public transportation programs designed for commuters to and from work activities in rural Georgia are virtually nonexistent in the job hinterland.
- Public transportation programs designed for an elderly and handicapped clientele in rural Georgia do not fit the full-day work activity model.

RECOMMENDATIONS

It is recommended that several actions be taken to impede the immobility/poverty/nonworker syndrome in rural Georgia and propel the mobility/personal income/work activity model in the job hinterland.

First, an advocacy role should be assumed by community development administrators and regional planners to enhance worker mobility, particularly now with the threat of increased transportation costs becoming a hindrance to work commuters.

Second, a determination should be made of the spatial dispersion relating nonworker and other potential employee residences to a proposed industrial or commercial activity. An integral part of that determination requires developing information on the incidence of nonworker immobility, as defined in this research, that exists within the activity hinterland. This approach would serve as the catalyst that weds the proposed activity to the community and, ultimately, propels the economic process for working and nonworking residents as well as for merchants and industrialists.

Third, limitations of the 1973 Federal-Aid Highway Act (*U.S. Code:* PL 93–87, 1974) pertaining to rural public transportation must be recognized. Section 147 established *only* demonstration programs for rural public transportation, and Section 301(g) 16(b) applied the urban model for the elderly and the handicapped to rural transportation conditions. These programs have been oversold as a panacea for solving rural mobility issues. Such is not the case. Officials thought that Section 147 programs would fill the transit gaps created by bus route abandonments of the common carriers and that Section 301 programs would provide equipment that could be utilized for the nonelderly and nonhandicapped. As mentioned previously in Chapters 2 and 5, elderly and handicapped programs operating on an eight-hour day do not fit the work activity time requirement. Additionally, intercity line-haul common carriers generally do not operate off the federal-aid system and surely not off the state-aid numbered system, where many of the nonworkers are believed to live. It is suggested, therefore, that elderly and handicapped programs not be used as a basis for work activity transportation programs. Furthermore, it is suggested that intercity line-haul operations be considered for what they are relative to the nonnetwork dweller: a partial service, at best, in a "split-mode" journey to work. It is recommended strongly that work activity transportation programs should either stand alone or — if economic necessity and policy constraints require a joint program — the work activity should dominate the responsible agency's operation. Departures and arrivals should be scheduled to meet the needs of work commuters so that their job hours are given first consideration when transportation priorities are set. Two economic purposes could be served by establishing priorities to meet worker mobility needs: (1) the public conveyance may be the mechanism that removes a recipient of transfer payments from the welfare rolls to a productive wage-earning role, and (2) part of the transportation program could be repaid by charges (fares) assessed to the new wage-earning commuter.

Fourth, explicit prohibitions regarding "labor standards" for transit-related labors are mandated under Section 13 of UMTA 1964 (*U.S. Code:* 1601, PL 88–365, 1976d, pp. 20 and 21). Subsection 13(c) expressly protects the rights and "interests of employees affected by such assistance" under this act. These rights include access to current and future benefits under collective bargaining agreements, pension programs, reduction-in-force recalls, training programs, and "jobs held harmless" because of worsening economic conditions. Implicitly, because rural cost of living is purportedly lower than urban, neither administrators, nor operators, nor constructors may expect that local wage rates and accompanying benefits are to be considered less than in the surrounding region.

Fifth, limits of demand-responsive service and/or paratransit should be reviewed carefully *prior* to implementation to mitigate obvious failures. These programs typically are funded through grants without anticipating how and why rider behavior may change over time. Some limitations include (1) extensive travel times that will "wear thin" for the rider if the job situation degenerates; (2) lengthy waiting times, whether with Dial-a-Ride (taxi) at the door or Hail-a-Ride (jitney) at the corner; (3) unsafe drivers in company van pools where a co-worker may be charged with driving responsibility; (4) equipment that has an uncomfortable design, such as school bus configurations utilized for large-framed adults; and (5) other limitations encountered in previous programs established in similar geographic, demographic, and economic areas and social and political environments.

Sixth, the concept of "New Volks for Poor Folks" — that is, a personalized automobile grant program — is technically practicable for a low-density area with a spatially dispersed population, as in the sample counties of this research (Maggied, 1979, p. 14). Such a program would provide carless families with low-cost vehicles that cost less than $2,000 per year (Maggied, 1979, p. 240).

This per annum cost is based on an average of the domestic "low-priced three" subcompacts (four-door) list-priced at $4,205 per unit amortized over three years. The price includes equipment such as AM radio and rear window defogger at no visible extra cost. Average annual operating expense amounts to $405. Operating costs are based on 15,000 travel miles per year. Maintenance and repairs are borne extra but considered minimal because of few accessories to service and extras to fix.

Economically this program is feasible, particularly if it were to remove a family from public assistance rolls (Maggied, 1979, p. 240). It is also cost effective because it eliminates the need to purchase minibuses that require operators, dispatchers, and garages. Moreover, personalized automobiles provide almost full-time mobility by being on call during time periods when public service is not operating.

The negative side of the personalized automobiles concept rests with the political aspect of such a program. It probably would be untenable, if not explosive, because of its "welfare" implications. Families who legally are above the contemporary poverty line may have more need for such grants than some who fall below, making the program difficult, if not impossible, to administer. Social and psychological problems could emerge also. The personalized automobile, if required to be uniform in every way — color, and the like — may create a stigma for the clientele. Uniformity often becomes a badge that tags the program recipient as someone less than acceptable in status to society.

Finally — other problems considered, such as lack of employment opportunities, untrained individuals, and socially less-developed people — it may behoove the public administrators and policy planners servicing such a clientele in remote geographical areas to accept the conditions for what they are. The focus of economic development activity generally is not toward lifting the poor from their deficient position but rather to enhance the economic base of the landowner, merchant, and industrialist. The poor may benefit from the fallout of the step-up process that inheres to new jobs created by incoming activities. This "step-up" concept was coined (Maggied, 1979, p. 242) around 1967 during various regional economic development analyses and innovated for the Coastal Plains Regional Commission about 1968; the Upper Great Lakes Regional Commission, about 1970; the Appalachian Regional Commission, about 1972; and the Ozarks Regional Commission, about 1978. The concept comports to the Reagan Administration's "filtering-down" process, but with this major difference: step-up is action oriented, while filtering-down is passive conditioning over the long run in time. Such passivity contradicts the "let's make it happen" attitude through unlimited opportunity and free choice of private enterprise in the exchange marketplace — a conflict of ideas, indeed. With tight public budgets, particularly in rural counties, it is difficult to imagine that funds would be available even if the polity were attuned affirmatively to providing personal transportation for the needy.

FINAL ANALYSIS

This research demonstrated that personal mobility was a limiting factor on personal income and work activity, particularly in rural areas and small places. A model was developed depicting the relationships between these parameters. Findings in other studies pertaining to the scope of this research were used to substantiate our hypothesis. The model was tested on two sample counties in rural Georgia, each located in diverse geophysical terrain. The data derived from the test indicate that the hypothesis is valid.

The findings suggest much more, however. Other variables pertaining to the parameter relationships of the model were analyzed also. The results of the analysis suggest that although the model as it is designed adds significantly to personal transportation theory, it is also an added link to economic development theory because it includes low-income workers as a significant, if not an equal, element in the foci of location factors rather than as a peripheral variable or nonentity. These additional links are not the end, however; they are the beginning of another avenue of research that I intend to pursue so that the elements of the poverty syndrome that are caused by immobility can be substantially diminished if not totally eliminated.

Assuredly, other inferences could be drawn from the data and analyses performed in this research. The findings suggest that this approach should be pursued to discover if other complex relationships impinge upon the mobility/personal income/work activity model. The model is valid, however, and can be applied as a minimum to all of Georgia's rural counties, if not to all rural counties across the nation.

AFTERWORD
John S. Hassell, Jr.

The research reported on in this publication results in very interesting policy implications for public administrators seeking to improve economic conditions because of its findings concerning the relationship between mobility and economic activity. The relationship between travel time and available time for economic activities is important for public policy concerning social assistance programs, also. Alternative transportation and mobility programs cannot be overlooked.

Historically, public policy has sought to improve the economic conditions of the poor through the development of labor-intensive, lower-skilled industries. Although these efforts have led to limited success, the conclusions of Dr. Maggied's research help us to understand better the failures that have occurred. Because of the lack of mobility, there has not been the

John S. Hassell, Jr., is the Federal Highway Administrator of the U.S. Department of Transportation's federal highway program. He is responsible for the overall direction, control, and evaluation of the $9 billion national highway program.

Prior to 1978, Mr. Hassell was chief of the Policy Planning Section of the Georgia Department of Transportation.

Mr. Hassell is a graduate of the Georgia Institute of Technology, with B.S. and M.S. degrees in civil engineering.

upgrading of jobs that was expected once the labor-intensive, lower-skilled industry had become established. In fact, in many regions of the country there now appears to have developed a continuing poverty syndrome related to the immobility of the working poor in rural areas.

Public policymakers should consider the mobility question in developing economic development plans for their areas. The one implicit locational decision matrix that did not consider labor input from a worker mobility standpoint should be analyzed carefully. If the policy decision is to go with labor-intensive, lower-skilled industry, the importance of locational considerations for labor mobility to participate in Dr. Maggied's step-up process is imperative.

Past public policy from the federal and state levels has emphasized the acquisition of economic activity for regions, with the explicit assumption that lower-income labor would be benefited implicitly. With the changing federal policies concerning economic development activity, the interrelationship of government and business becomes important for public policymakers. As state and regional officials seek to maximize the employment activities that result from their economic development programs, the importance of policy correlations with transportation investments becomes obvious from this research. With the limited resources for economic development, coupled with the changing federal transportation policies under the new administration, the decision-making options available to state and local officials should increase; furthermore, an additional factor that decisionmakers should become aware of rests with the mobility implications of economic development activities.

As the research points out, the interrelation between time budget and life-support activity is often overlooked, if considered important at all. The transportation implications of the time budget concept is quite important from a policy perspective. One of the major economic policies for developing areas is oriented around the accumulation of capital resources to achieve the "take-off point" in economic development activity. If a major portion of the individual's time budget is consumed in satisfying mobility requirements, and the life-support time is likewise substantial — as is often the case for the poor — the remaining time available for productive activities is limited. This greatly diminishes the accumulation of capital resources and further frustrates individual as well as regional economic development.

Transportation managers and economic policymakers must take into account these factors. Again, it must be emphasized that the use of the time budget concept, as suggested in this research, can be very helpful to the policymaker.

Traditional economic development theory points to the importance of educational and training programs in providing trained work forces to take advantage of economic activity opportunities. If one adds these to the time budget, which already contains such life-support activities as subsistence farming and a large time allocation for mobility purposes to get to existing job opportunities, it can be seen quite readily that the policymaker's efforts to further the economic welfare of the individual can be easily frustrated and may be a major factor in some of the program failures that have been observed.

From a transportation perspective there are several policy issues that must be included in transportation planning for less-developed areas. Mobility schemes for the economically disadvantaged become a critical factor in education and training, economic development efforts, and social programs. The success of these policies in achieving improved life circumstances for poor and rural residents becomes dependent upon the transportation policies concurrently developed.

Many states and regions have developed highway systems that now provide a high level of access to relatively remote areas. This research suggests that this level of access has not been translated into mobility for many citizens, particularly along byways in the hinterlands. With public policies shifting away from social and economic development programs, longer-term policy implications from immobility concerns become even more significant.

To understand better the consequence of changes in rural development policy, it might be well to look at a few possible directions that can be expected from the new administration in Washington. If the previously announced direction of reduction and even elimination of economic development programs is pursued, job opportunities in rural areas will be constrained even further over what could have been expected. When this reduction or elimination is added to the already significant constraint of lengthy work trips necessary for the rural poor, the social cost of reduction in these programs becomes more obvious.

Coupled with the decreases in economic development efforts, the administration is proposing major reductions in transportation programs. Areas specifically outlined in proposals before Congress are a reduction in, or the elimination of, the Section 147 Rural Public Transportation Grant program under the Urban Mass Transit Act of 1978 and a reduction and eventual elimination of much of the Federal-Aid Highway program in other than the interstate category. These initiatives will compound further the plight of the poor in less-developed areas and, if not supplemented by major efforts on the part of state and local governments, will result in a reduction of mobility both for individuals on personal trips and for those on trips connected with economic and industrial activities.

These actions come at a time when population increases are occurring in nonurban parts of the country, increasing the burden on taxpayers for education and safety as well as transportation and economic development activities. States are hard pressed, particularly in the transportation area, as increases in crude oil prices and the introduction and procurement of more fuel-efficient vehicles have significantly decreased funds available to most state highway agencies. The pressing chore of maintaining the existing highway systems in a passable condition is stretching many state highway funds budgets beyond the limits of endurance.

Dr. Maggied's research demonstrates the increasingly difficult problems created by a lack of mobility for the rural poor. When one looks at the challenges of bringing these citizens into the economic mainstream of the nation, it becomes obvious that solving their problems of transportation disadvantage is equally important to any of the other factors in providing for their occupational uplift.

During much of the history of transportation in this nation, it has been a major national goal to improve mobility for all citizens and goods. The correlation and symbiosis between economic advantage and transportation have been demonstrated and accepted throughout the history of the nation. Although the problems that Dr. Maggied identifies have been with us for generations, the means and wherewithal to solve them are now available to us.

As Dr. Bivens pointed out in his Foreword, there has been a lack of coordination in comprehensive development to provide rural mobility. It is hoped that the work begun by Dr. Maggied will provide renewed emphasis in this major policy area. As we search for new direction during the remainder of this century, it is crucial that policy developers consider the entire range of program activities available to address our nation's problems.

However, if the new administration proceeds with its enunciated federal policy direction, it only can be concluded that it will work to the disadvantage of poor residents in rural areas. The resources of transportation will be stretched beyond the point where they can respond to the conditions and needs for transportation services in rural areas.

One can speculate that the long-term net outcome of the policy directions being pursued at present in Washington will result in less transportation accessibility for the poor in most rural areas and a decrease in job options, leading to further constraints on the social, economic, and even physical well-being of poor rural citizens.

One has only to look at recent reductions in intercity bus service in many states to observe the inability of states and local governments to deal with this reduction in transportation and to realize that state and local governments are incapable of funding such programs. Moreover, they lack the legal tools to deal with rural mobility problems without federal assistance.

However, given the present federal administration policy, it appears un-likely that there will be any significant federal assistance for these areas in the near future.

Mobility for the rural poor has been shown by this research to be a critical aspect of all economic and social planning and highly relevant to transportation development in less-developed areas. Dr. Maggied's research and experience provide us with a better understanding of the interaction of transportation mobility with the economic and social conditions of the poor in many areas of this country. Further investigation on this complex interac-tion, as Dr. Maggied is doing, should help to define better the parameters that public policymakers must encounter when attempting to provide for economic development and improved mobility.

REFERENCES

Alex, Robert P. 1974. "State-of-the-Art Demand-Responsive Transportation."
   Demand-Responsive Systems Services. Special Report 154. Washington, D.C.:
   Transportation Research Board, National Research Council.
Appalachian Redevelopment Act of 1965. 1966. Public Law 89-4, 79 STAT 4, Vols.
   1 and 2. *U.S. Code: Legislative & Administrative News*. St. Paul, Minn., and
   Brooklyn, N.Y.: West Publishing Company and Edward Thompson Company.
Appalachian Regional Development Act Amendments of 1967. 1968. Public Law
   80-103, 81 STAT 257, Vol. 2. *U.S. Code: Legislative & Administrative News*. St.
   Paul, Minn., and Brooklyn, N.Y.: West Publishing Company and Charles
   Thompson Company.
Area Planning and Development Commissions, Georgia. 1976. Field visitations,
   October.
Area Redevelopment Act of 1961. 1962. Public Law 87-27, 75 STAT 47, Vols. 1 and
   2. *U.S. Code: Congressional & Administrative News*. St. Paul, Minn., and
   Brooklyn, N.Y: West Publishing Company.
Arkansas Highway Commission. 1979. "Facts and Figures: State Highway System,
   Calendar Year 1977." *33rd Biennial Report, 1977-78*. Little Rock, Ark. Informa-
   tion transmitted by George Bolineau, senior planning coordinator, during tele-
   phone conversation, April 15.
Asin, Ruth H., and Svercl, Paul C. 1974. "Automobile Ownership." *Nationwide
   Personal Transportation Study*. Report No. 11. U.S. Department of Transporta-

149

tion/Federal Highway Administration, Program Management Division, Office of Highway Planning.

Atlanta Regional Commission. 1976. "Transportation Needs of the Handicapped and Elderly Populations of the Atlanta Region." ARC staff working paper. Atlanta, ARC review draft, May.

Automobile Facts and Figures. 1968. Detroit: Automobile Manufacturers Association, Inc.

Batchelder, Alan B. 1966. *The Economics of Poverty.* Introduction to Economics Series. New York: John Wiley & Sons.

Bates, John W. 1970. "Comprehensive Planning for Rural Regions: A Case Study (The Slash Pine Experience)." GHD Research Assistance Project No. 2–70, special report. Atlanta: State Highway Department of Georgia, Planning and Operations Research Section, Division of Highway Planning, in cooperation with U.S. Department of Transportation, Federal Highway Administration.

Berne, Eric. 1961. *Transactional Analysis in Psychotherapy.* San Francisco: Castle Books.

Berry, Brian J. L. 1967. *Geography of Market Centers and Retail Distribution.* Englewood Cliffs, N.J.: Prentice-Hall.

Biddle, William W., and Biddle, Loureide J. 1965. *The Community Development Process.* New York: Holt, Rinehart & Winston.

Bivens, William. 1979–1981. Senior Fellow for Rural Policy, National Governors' Association. Personal conversations, Washington, D.C., and Atlanta, January 25, 1980, and September 15, 1980, respectively. Telephone conversations, September 1979–March 1981.

Bolineau, George. 1974–1979. Senior coordinator, Statewide Planning Office, Georgia Department of Transportation. Intermittent conversations.

Bowles, Gladys K., and Beale, Calvin L. 1980. "Commuting and Migration Status in Nonmetro Areas." Reprinted from *Agricultural Economics Research*, U.S. Department of Agriculture, Economic Development Division, ESCS. Vol. 32, No. 3. Washington, D.C., July 1980.

Brooks, Sueanne. 1976–1977. Program specialist, Department of Health, Education, and Welfare, Region IV. Personal conversations, 1976–1977. Sixth Annual Transportation Conference for the Elderly and Handicapped, Atlanta, November 1976; St. Petersburg Beach, Fl., December 1977.

Brown, E. H. Phelps. 1962. *The Economics of Labor.* New Haven, Conn., Yale University Press.

Bruton, Robert. 1977. Chief, Rural Transportation, U.S. Department of Transportation, Office of University Research, Office of the Secretary. Personal interview, April.

Bryce, Herrington J. 1979. *Planning Smaller Cities.* Lexington, Mass.: Lexington Books.

Burkhardt, Jon, and Eby, Charles L. 1969. *Transportation Needs of the Rural Poor.* Prepared for the U.S. Department of Transportation, Federal Highway Administration. Washington, D.C.: Resource Management Corporation.

Busacker, Robert G., and Saaty, Thomas L. 1965. *Finite Graphs and Networks.* New York: McGraw-Hill Book Company.

Bush, Al. 1977–1978. Certification Officer, Georgia Public Service Commission. Telephone conversation, November 16, 1977, and June 1, 1978.

Butts, James. 1972. "Programs for the Transit Dependent in Rural Areas." *Conference on Transportation and Human Needs in the '70's: The Second Phase.* U.S. Department of Transportation, June 19–21.

Byrne, Bernard F., and Neumann, Edward S. No date. "Feasibility of Developing Low-Cost Measures of Demand for Rural Public Transportation." USDOT Office of University Research Contract (DOT–OS–50127).

Byrne, Bernard F.; Neumann, Edward S.; Royce, Blaine M.; and Leung, Edwin P. No date. "Development of High Resolution Regression Models for Forecasting Demand along Rural Transit Routes."

"Car Shoppers Kick Cost — And Buy." 1977. *Atlanta Constitution,* November 27, Vol. 128, No. 52.

Carstens, R. L., et al. 1975. *Transit Assistant Programs for Iowa.* Ames: Iowa State University, Engineering Research Institute.

Clemente, Frank, and Summers, Gene F. 1975. "The Journey to Work of Rural Industrial Employees." *Social Forces* (September):217.

Coates, Vary T. 1974. *Revitalization of Small Communities: Transportation Options.* Prepared for the U.S. Department of Transportation, Office of the Secretary, Office of University Research, Washington, D.C.

Coates, Vary T., and Weiss, Ernest. 1975. *Revitalization of Small Communities: Transportation Options.* Prepared for the U.S. Department of Transportation, Office of the Secretary, Office of University Research, Washington, D.C.

Comrey, Andrew L. 1973. *A First Course in Factor Analysis.* New York: Academic Press.

Crain, John L. 1972. "Transportation Problems of Transit Dependent Persons — A Status Report." *Conference on Transportation and Human Needs in the '70's: The Second Phase.* U.S. Department of Transportation, June 19–21.

Davis, F. W., and Oen, K. 1977. *Solving Public Passenger Transportation Problems: A Need for Policy Reorientation.* Prepared for the U.S. Department of Transportation, Office of the Secretary, Office of University Research, Knoxville, University of Tennessee, Transportation Center, January.

Dayton, Sam. 1978. Executive Director, Georgia Mountains Area Planning and Development Commission. Telephone conversation, October.

Dean, Donald, and Drosdat, Herb. 1976. "Transit Needs in Small California Communities." Sacramento, Calif., Department of Transportation, Division of Mass Transportation and Division of Planning, Technical Research Branch, September.

DeJong, Gordon F., and Sell, Ralph R. 1977. "Population Redistribution, Migration, and Residential Preference." *Annals of the American Academy of Political and Social Science* 429 (January):130–44.

Demonstration Cities and Metropolitan Development Act of 1966. 1967. Public Law 89–754, 80 STAT 1255, Vol. 3. *U.S. Code: Congressional & Administrative News.* St. Paul, Minn., and Brooklyn, N.Y.: West Publishing Company and Charles Thompson Company.

"Detroit Report." 1976. *Popular Science* (December).

Dickey, John W. 1973. *Rural Public Transportation Needs and Recommendations.* Prepared for the Virginia Metropolitan Areas Transportation Study Committee. Blacksburg; Va.: Center for Urban and Regional Studies, Virginia Polytechnical Institute and State University.

————. 1977. *A Transportation Credits Program for Smaller Cities and Rural Areas.* Blacksburg, Va.: Center for Urban and Regional Studies, Virginia Polytechnical Institute and State University.

Dillman, Don A., and Tremblay, Kenneth R., Jr. 1977. "The Quality of Life in Rural America." *Annals of the American Academy of Political and Social Science* 429 (January):115–29.

Economic Opportunity Act of 1964. 1965. Public Law 88–452, 78 STAT 508, Vols. 1 and 2. *U.S. Code: Congressional & Administrative News.* St. Paul, Minn., and Brooklyn, N.Y.: West Publishing Company and Edward Thompson Company.

Economic Opportunity Amendments of 1966. 1967. Public Law 89–794, 80 STAT 1451, Vol. 3. *U.S. Code: Congressional & Administrative News.* St. Paul, Minn., and Brooklyn, N.Y.: West Publishing Company and Charles Thompson Company.

Economic Opportunity Admendments of 1967. 1968. Public Law 90–222, 81 STAT 672, Vols. 1 and 2. *U.S. Code: Congressional & Administrative News.* St. Paul, Minn., and Brooklyn, N.Y.: West Publishing Company and Charles Thompson Company.

Elliot, Jesse. 1978. Director, Research and Statistics, Georgia Department of Education. Telephone conversation, Atlanta, October 14.

Ellul, Jacques. 1964. *The Technological Society.* New York: Vintage Books.

Executive Office of the President. 1979. "The White House Rural Development Initiatives: Improving Transportation in Rural America." Washington, D.C.: U.S. Government Printing Office.

Executive Order of the President No. 11647. 1973. "Federal Regional Councils." *Federal Register,* Vol. 37, F. R. 3167, February 10, 1972. *U.S. Code: Congressional & Administrative News.* Vol. 3. St. Paul, Minn.: West Publishing Company.

Eyestone, Robert. 1972. *Political Economy: Politics and Policy Analysis.* Chicago: Markham Publishing Company.

Falcocchio, John C., and Cantilli, Edmund J. 1974. *Transportation and the Disadvantaged.* Lexington, Mass.: D. C. Heath.

Farmer, Joseph T. 1976. "The Socioeconomic Impact of the Mountain Parkway and KY 15." Lexington, Ky.: Kentucky Bureau of Highways, Division of Research.

————. 1979. Kentucky Bureau of Highways, Division of Research, Lexington, Ky. Telephone conversation, September 9.

Farmer, Joseph T., and Pigman, Jerry G. 1974a. " 'Before' Evaluation of Economic Growth Center Developmental Highway (KY 55, Campbellsville-Lebanon)." Lexington, Ky.: Kentucky Bureau of Highways, Division of Research.

————. 1974b. " 'Before' Evaluation of Economic Growth Center Developmental Highway (US 25E: Corbin-Barbourville)." Lexington, Ky.: Kentucky Bureau of Highways, Division of Research.

Federal-Aid Highway Act of 1968. 1969. Public Law 90–495, 82 STAT 815, Vol. 2.

U.S. Code: Congressional & Administrative News. St. Paul, Minn., and Brooklyn, N.Y.: West Publishing Company and Charles Thompson Company.

Federal-Aid Highway Act of 1973. 1974. Public Law 93-87, 87 STAT 250, Vol. 1. *U.S. Code: Congressional & Administrative News.* St. Paul, Minn.: West Publishing Company.

Ferman, Louis A. 1969. *Job Development for the Hard to Employ.* Policy Papers in Human Resources and Industrial Relations, No. 11. University of Michigan and Wayne State University.

Fulton, Dr. Philip. 1978. U.S. Bureau of Census, Population Division, Suitland, Md. Telephone conversation, February 7.

Garrity, Dave. 1974–1978. Senior transportation planner, Georgia Office of Planning and Budget, Planning Division. Personal and telephone conversations.

Georgia. 1973. Department of Transportation. "Yellow Book." *Standard Specifications for Road and Bridge Construction.* Atlanta.

———. 1974. Office of the Governor, Planning Division. *Executive Summary: Development Policy Plan.* Atlanta.

———. 1975. Office of Planning and Budget, State Data Center. *County Population Estimates: 1974.* Atlanta.

———. 1976. Department of Transportation. "Impact of an Expanding Transportation Network on Potential Economic Development Location in the North Georgia Area." Research and Development Bureau, Office of Materials and Tests. Forest Park, Ga.

———. 1977a. Department of Human Resources, Division of Family and Children Services Statistical Unit. "Consolidated Statement of Public Assistance Money Payments." Computer printout transmitted by Mack Cawthon, Atlanta, November 10.

———. 1977b. Department of Labor, Division of Research and Statistics. "1975 Labor Force and Unemployment Estimates of Annual Averages." Transmitted by Patricia Cobb, Atlanta, October 3.

———. 1977c. Department of Transportation, Division of Planning and Programming. "Baker County," *General Highway Map.* Atlanta.

———. 1977d. Department of Transportation, Division of Planning and Programming. "Dawson County," *General Highway Map.* Atlanta.

———. 1977e. Department of Transportation, Planning Data Services Section. "Mileage of Public Roads in Georgia Classified by Highway District, County, Surface Type, and System." DPP Statistical Report No. 441–D–77. Atlanta.

———. 1977–1978. Office of Planning and Budget, Management Review Division, "Plan A," 1975 Population Estimates. Data Center special calculation. Transmitted to the Georgia Department of Transportation, Division of Planning and Programming. Atlanta.

———. 1978a. Department of Industry and Trade. "Baker County." *EDP: Economic Development Profile.* Individual county brochures, transportation.

———. 1978b. Department of Transportation, Division of Planning and Programming. "1973 Travel Time Data." Computer printout work sheet transmitted by George Bolineau, Senior Planning Coordinator, Decatur, Ga., January 10.

————. 1979. Department of Industry and Trade. "Dawson County." *EDP: Economic Development Profile*. Individual county brochures, transportation.

————. 1980. Department of Transportation, Planning Data Services. "Georgia Area Planning and Development Commissions, 1979." Atlanta.

————. 1981. Department of Community Affairs, Community Development Division. "Growth Areas and Growth Corridors." Official representation transmitted by Steve Rieck, Deputy Director, Atlanta, March 19.

Georgia Mountains Area Planning and Development Commission. 1976. "GAMTRAN." Project proposed to the Federal Highway Administration, Gainesville, Ga.

Gess, Dr. Larry. 1973–1978. Governor's advisor on education, Planning Division, Office of Planning and Budget, State of Georgia. Periodic personal discussions.

Getzels, Judith, and Thurow, Charles, eds. 1979. *Rural and Small Town Planning*. Chicago and Washington, D.C.: Planners Press, American Planning Association.

Gill, Richard T. 1963. *Economic Development: Past and Present*. Englewood Cliffs, N.J.: Prentice-Hall.

Gilstrap, Jack. 1981. Director, American Public Transit Association. Interview in panel discussion on "MacNeil/Lehrer Report," *PBS*. WETA Television, Athens/Atlanta, Ga., February 26.

Goldmark, Peter. 1976. Cited in "Executive Summary," *Socioeconomic Impact of Investment in Transportation and Communication*. Final report by Carol Lee Hilewick, Edward J. Deak, Kay K. Kahls, and Edward Heinze. Sponsored by the U.S. Department of Transportation, Urban Mass Transportation Administration, Office of R&D Policy (TST–10). Washington, D.C.: U.S. Government Printing Office through National Technical Information Service.

Goldschmidt, Neil, 1980. Secretary of Transportation. "Intercity Bus Service in Small Communities," *Executive Summary*. Washington, D.C.: U.S. Department of Transportation, Office of the Secretary.

Gould, P. 1969. *Spatial Diffusion*. Commission on College Geography, Association of American Geographers. Washington, D.C.: AAG. Cited in Mosely et al. (1970).

Grant, Vance. 1978. Director, Research and Statistics, National Center for Educational Statistics. Telephone conversation, Washington, D.C., October 16.

Gurin, Douglas B. 1976. "Paratransit in Small Communities and Non-urbanized Areas." *Paratransit*. Special Report 164. Proceedings of a conference held November 9–12, 1975. Conducted by the Transportation Research Board and sponsored by the Urban Mass Transportation Administration. Washington, D.C.: Transportation Research Board, National Research Council.

Gutenschwager, Gerald A. 1973. "The Time-Budget-Activity Systems Perspective in Urban Research and Planning." *AIP Journal* (November).

Haggett, Peter, and Chorley, Richard. 1969. *Network Analysis in Geography*. New York: St. Martins Press.

Hauser, Edwin W.; Rooks, Elizabeth; Johnston, Steven A.; and Gillivray, Lois May. 1975. "The Use of Existing Facilities for Transporting Disadvantaged Residents of Rural Areas." *Guide for Transportation Providers*. Prepared for So-cioeconomic Studies, Office of Program and Policy Planning, Federal Highway Administration, Research Triangle Institute, Research Triangle Park, N.C.

Hoover, Edgar. 1948. *The Location of Economic Activity*. New York: McGraw-Hill Book Company.

Housing Act of 1959. 1960. Public Law 86-372, 73 STAT 654. *U.S. Code: Congressional & Administrative News*. St. Paul, Minn., and Brooklyn, N.Y.: West Publishing Company.

Housing Act of 1961. 1962. Public Law 87-70, 75 STAT 149. *U.S. Code: Congressional & Administrative News*. St. Paul, Minn., and Brooklyn, N.Y.: West Publishing Company.

Housing Act of 1964. 1965. Public Law 88-560, 78 STAT 769, Vol. 1. *U.S. Code: Congressional & Administrative News*. St. Paul, Minn., and Brooklyn, N.Y.: West Publishing Company and Edward Thompson Company.

Housing and Community Development Act of 1974. 1975. Public Law 93-382, 88 STAT 633, Vol. 1. *U.S. Code: Congressional & Administrative News*. St. Paul, Minn.: West Publishing Company.

Housing and Community Development Amendments Act of 1979. 1980. Public Law 96-153, 93 STAT 1101, Vol. 1. *U.S. Code: Congressional & Administrative News*. St. Paul, Minn.: West Publishing Company.

Housing and Urban Development Act of 1968. 1969. Public Law 90-448, 82 STAT 476, Vols. 1 and 2. *U.S. Code: Congressional & Administrative News*. St. Paul, Minn., and Brooklyn, N.Y.: West Publishing Company and Charles Thompson Company.

Housing and Urban Development Act of 1969. 1970. Public Law 91-152, 83 STAT 379, Vol. 2. *U.S. Code: Congressional & Administrative News*. St. Paul, Minn., and Brooklyn, N.Y.: West Publishing Company and Charles Thompson Company.

Hughes, Johnathon. 1965. *The Vital Few*. Boston: Houghton Mifflin Company.

Hunker, Henry. 1974. *Industrial Development*. Lexington, Mass.: Lexington Books.

The Impact of Transportation on the Delivery of Human Services. 1976. Commonwealth of Virginia. Prepared by Office of the Governor, Secretary of Transportation, and the Division of State Planning and Community Affairs; financed by the Urban Mass Transportation Administration.

Interplan, Incorporated. 1974. "The Socio-Economic Consequences of the Appalachian Highway on the North Georgia Area." Georgia Department of Transportation Contract Research Project No. 5-73, in cooperation with the Appalachian Regional Commission. Final Report. Boston.

Isard, Walter. 1975. *Introduction to Regional Science*. Englewood Cliffs, N.J.: Prentice-Hall.

Issues in Statewide Transportation Planning. 1974a. "Workshop 3A: Systems Planning and Programming Methodology: Passenger Travel." TRB Special Report 146, report of a conference held February 21-24 at Williamsburg, Va. Transportation Research Board, National Research Council.

————. 1974b. "Workshop 4: State and Regional Development." TRB Special

Report 146, report of a conference held February 21–24 at Williamsburg, Va. Transportation Research Board, National Research Council.

Kaye, Ira. 1976a. "Mobility in Rural America — Need for Public Transportation for People." Washington, D.C.: Rural Housing Alliance and Rural America, Inc., Conference Working Paper No. 1, Transportation.

———. 1976b. "Rural Transportation: Problems and Perspectives." *Proceedings of the First National Conference on Rural Transportation.* U.S. Department of Transportation, Office of University Research and Technology Sharing Program, North Carolina A&T State University, Transportation Research Board, National Council on the Transportation Disadvantaged.

———. 1977. Telephone conversations and letter correspondence. Chevy Chase, Md., May 15 and 17.

Kidder, Alice E., and Saltzman, Arthur. 1972. "Transportation of the Autoless Worker in a Small City." Greensboro: Transportation Institute, North Carolina Agricultural and Technical State University.

Kimley-Horn and Associates, Inc. 1975a. "Planning and Development Program for Mass Transportation Services and Facilities for the Elderly and Handicapped." Prepared for the Georgia Department of Transportation, Bureau of Mass Transportation, Raleigh, N.C.

———. 1975b. "Statewide Study of Transportation for Tennessee's Elderly." Prepared for the Bureau of Mass Transit, Tennessee Department of Transportation, in Cooperation with the Tennessee Commission on Aging, Nashville, Tenn.

———. 1976. "Coastal Georgia Rural Public Transportation Study." Prepared for the Coastal Area Planning and Development Commission, Jacksonville, Fl.

Kirby, Ronald. 1975. "Paratransit, A State-of-the-Art Overview." *Paratransit.* Special Report No. 164. Conference proceedings, sponsored by the Urban Mass Transportation Administration, Washington, D.C., November 9–12.

Kohler, Heinz. 1968. *Scarcity Challenged: An Introduction to Economics.* New York: Holt, Rinehart & Winston.

Kohn, Richard. 1981. "Morning Report," *CBS News.* WRNG Radio, Atlanta, March 21, 8:10 A.M.

Kuralt, Charles. 1981. "Sunday Morning," *CBS News.* WAGA Television, Atlanta, March 1, 9:05 A.M.

Laitila, E. E.; Salmon, R.; Maggied, H. S.; Hamilton, H. R.; and Duncan, J. W. 1967. *Environmental Study of Logan, McDowell, and Mingo Counties, West Virginia, and Pike County, Kentucky.* Prepared for U.S. Army Corps of Engineers, Huntington District.

Lamb, Danny. 1975–1979. Senior planner, Statewide Planning Office, Georgia Department of Transportation. Periodic discussions, Atlanta.

Lemly, James. 1958. "Expressway Influence on Land Use and Value." Prepared for the State Highway Department of Georgia, Division of Planning. Atlanta: Bureau of Business and Economic Research, School of Business Administration, Georgia State University.

Lester, Richard A., ed. 1968. "A Comprehensive Employment and Manpower Policy." *Labor: Readings on Major Issues.* New York: Random House.

Levine, Arnold L. 1977. "Intercity Bus Service to Rural and Small Urban Communities." *Proceedings of the National Symposium on Transportation for Agriculture and Rural America*. Washington, D.C.: U.S. Department of Transportation, Office of Rural Transportation.

Liebow, Elliot. 1967. *Talley's Corner*. Boston: Little, Brown & Company.

Lynch, Paul. 1975. Georgia Department of Revenues, Office of Research and Statistics. Telephone conversation, Atlanta.

"MacNeil/Lehrer Reports." 1981. Discussion of issue on Boston Metropolitan Transit Authority reported in audit by General Accounting Office. *PBS*. WETA Television, Athens/Atlanta, February 23.

Maggied, Hal S. 1967a. "Human Resources in 4 Appalachian Counties," for the Huntington District, Corps of Engineers. Columbus, Ohio: Battelle Columbus Laboratories.

———. 1967b. "Transportation in 4 Appalachian Counties," for the Huntington District, Corps of Engineers. Columbus, Ohio: Battelle Columbus Laboratories.

———. 1974. "Determinants of Population Change and Commuting Patterns in the State of Georgia Between 1970 and 1972." Georgia Governor's Office, Planning and Budget Divisions. Atlanta.

———. 1976. "Critical Needs in Georgia's Statewide Transportation System." Memorandum report to F. L. Breen, Jr., director, Georgia Department of Transportation. Atlanta.

———. 1978a. "Georgia's Critical Rural Public Transportaton Needs." (Abridgment.) *Transportation Research Record* No. 661. Washington, D.C.: National Research Council.

———. 1978b. "Identification of Rural Georgia's Transportation Disadvantaged." *Transportation for the Elderly and Handicapped: Programs and Problems*. U.S. Department of Transportation, Research and Special Programs Administration, Transportation Systems Center. Cambridge, Mass.

———. 1979. "Transportation Options for the Mobility Disadvantaged in Rural Georgia." Unpublished doctoral dissertation, University of Georgia, Athens.

———. 1981. "Georgia: Commuting Problems in Rural Areas." *Programs and Problems, No. 2: Transportation for the Elderly and Handicapped*. U.S. Department of Transportation, Office of Technology Transfer, Transportation Systems Center. Cambridge, Mass.

———. Maggied, Hal S.; Pannell, Clifton W.; Farkas, Z. Andrew; and Wheeler, James O. 1977. "Land Use and Intra-Regional Transportation: An Appalachian Georgia Analysis." Transportation Research Board, National Research Council. Department of Geography, University of Georgia.

Maggied, Hal S.; Pannell, Clifton W.; Farkas, Z. Andrew; and Wheeler, James O. 1977. "Land Use and Intra-Regional Transportation: An Appalachian Georgia Analysis." Transportation Research Board, National Research Council. Department of Geography, University of Georgia.

Manpower Development and Training Act of 1961. 1962. Public Law 87–415, 76 STAT 23, Vol. 1. *U.S. Code: Congressional Administrative News*. St. Paul, Minn.: West Publishing Company.

Manpower Development and Training Act of 1962. 1963. Public Law 88–214, 77
  STAT 422. *U.S. Code: Congressional & Administrative News.* St. Paul, Minn.,
  and Brooklyn, N.Y.: West Publishing Company.
Manpower Development and Training Act Amendments of 1966. 1967. Public Law
  89–792, 80 STAT 1434, Vol. 3. *U.S. Code: Congressional & Administrative
  News.* St. Paul, Minn., and Brooklyn, N.Y.: West Publishing Company and
  Charles Thompson Company.
Marshall, Alfred. 1961. *Principles of Economics,* 9th ed. New York: Macmillan.
McKelvey, Douglas. 1979. Policy analyst, National Transportation Task Force.
  Personal conversations at the Seventh National Transportation Conference for
  the Elderly and Handicapped, Orlando, Fl., December 10.
McManus, Robert H. 1972. "Financing Public Transportation." *Issues in Public
  Transportation.* Special Report No. 144. National Research Council, Transporta-
  tion Research Board, Highway Research Board. Proceedings of a conference held
  at Henniker, N.H., July 9–12.
Meyer, John R., and Kain, John F. 1968. *Interrelationships of Transportation and
  Poverty: Summary of Conference on Transportation and Poverty.* Prepared for
  the American Academy of Arts and Sciences, Brookline, Mass., June 7.
Meyer, John R.; Peck, Merton J.; Stenason, John; and Swick, Charles. 1960. *The
  Economics of Competition in the Transportation Industries.* Cambridge, Mass.:
  Harvard University Press.
"Migration and the Labor Force: Prospects." 1968. *Monthly Labor Review* (March).
  Washington, D.C.: U.S. Department of Labor.
Millar, William. 1977. Pennsylvania Department of Transportation, Bureau of Ad-
  vance Planning. Telephone conversation, November 10.
Millard, Ray. 1981. Advisory consultant, World Bank, Highway Engineering De-
  partment. Telephone conversation, Washington, D.C., February 13.
Mosely, M. J.; Harman, R. G.; Coles, O. B.; and Spencer, M. B. 1977. *Rural
  Transport and Accessibility.* Norwich, Eng: Centre of East Anglian Studies,
  University of East Anglia.
Myers, Sumner. 1968. "Personal Transportation for the Poor." *Conference on
  Poverty and Transportation.* Springfield, Va.: Clearing House for Scientific and
  Technical Information.
National Mass Transportation Act of 1974. 1975. Public Law 93–503, 88 STAT
  1561, Vols. 1 and 3. *U.S. Code: Congressional & Administrative News.* St. Paul,
  Minn., and Brooklyn, N.Y.: West Publishing Company and Charles Thompson.
National Rural Center. 1979. "Rural Public Transportation," Vol. 1, No. 5.
  Washington, D.C.
National Rural Center. 1980. "Rural Community Development," Vol. 2, No. 3.
  Washington, D.C.
Nemmers, Erwin Esser. 1966. *Dictionary of Economics and Business.* Totowa,
  N.J.: Littlefield, Adams & Company.
Neumann, Edward S., and Byrne, Bernard F. Undated. "A Poisson Model of Rural
  Transit Ridership."

"1975 Survey of Buying Power." 1975. *Sales Management & Marketing Magazine,* Vol. 115, No. 2.

Nobel, Brian. 1972. "Comments." *Conference on Transportation and Human Needs in the '70's: The Second Phase.* U.S. Department of Transportation, June 19–21.

North, Robert C.; Holsti, Ole R.; Zaninovich, M. George; and Zinnes, Dina A. 1963. *Content Analysis: Handbooks for Research in Political Behavior.* James A. Robinson, ed. Evanston, Ill.: Northwestern University Press.

Ochojna, A. D., and Brownlee, A. T. 1972. "Simple Indices for Diagnosing Rural Public Transport Problems." *Traffic Engineering and Control.* London: Printer Hall.

Ornati, Oscar. 1969. *Transportation Needs of the Poor.* New York: Praeger Publishers.

Orshansky, Mollie. 1972. "Counting the Poor: Another Look at the Poverty Profile." In Louis A. Ferman, Joyce L. Kronbluh, and Alan Haber, eds., *Poverty in America: A Book of Readings.* Ann Arbor: University of Michigan Press.

Owen, Wilfred. 1972. *The Accessible City.* Washington, D.C.: Brookings Institution.

———. 1976. *Transportation for Cities.* Washington, D.C.: Brookings Institution.

Paaswell, Robert E., and Recker, Wilfred W. 1974. "Location of the Carless." *Transportation Research Record.* Washington, D.C.: Transportation Research Board, National Research Council.

———. 1976. *Problems of the Carless.* Prepared for the U.S. Department of Transportation, Office of the Secretary and Office of University Research. Buffalo, N.Y.

Parham, Jim. 1977. Commissioner, Georgia Department of Human Resources. Interview, WSB Radio. Atlanta, January 27.

Peirce, Neal R. 1979. "Learning from Cities." *Transatlantic Perspectives,* Vol. 1. Washington, D.C.: The German Marshall Fund of the United States.

Public Works Acceleration Act of 1962. 1963. Public Law 87–658, 76 STAT 541, Vol. 2. *U.S. Code: Congressional & Administrative News.* St. Paul, Minn.: West Publishing Company.

Randill, Alice; Greenhalfh, Helen; and Samson, Elizabeth. 1973. "Mode of Transportation and Personal Characteristics of Tripmakers." *Nationwide Personal Transportation Study.* Report No. 9. U.S. Department of Transportation, Federal Highway Administration.

Regional Development Act of 1975. 1976. Public Law 94–188, STAT 1078, Vol. 2. *U.S. Code: Congressional & Administrative News.* St. Paul, Minn., and Brooklyn, N.Y.: West Publishing Company and Charles Thompson Company.

Reichart, Barbara K. 1975. "Nonurbanized Public Transportation: A Federal Perspective." *Paratransit.* Conference on Paratransit, Williamsburg, Va. Washington, D.C.: Transportation Research Board, National Research Council.

Reichman, Shalom. 1976. "Conceptual Problems in Evaluation of Travel Time." *Transportation Research Record 587.* Washington, D.C.: National Research Council.

Rein, Martin. 1972. "Problems in the Definition and Measurement of Poverty." *Poverty in America: A Book of Readings.* Ann Arbor: University of Michigan Press.

Reynolds. L. G. 1951. *The Structure of the Labor Market.* New Haven, Conn.: Yale University Press.

Robbins, Lionel. 1940. *An Essay on the Nature and Significance of Economic Science.* London: Macmillan.

Ronan, William. 1972. "Address to Plenary Session." *Conference on Transportation and Human Needs in the '70's: The Second Phase.* U.S. Department of Transportation, June 19–21.

Ross, Howard R. 1972. "New Urban Transportation Technology and the Transit Dependent." Paper prepared for the *Conference on Transportation and Human Needs in the '70's: The Second Phase.* Washington, D.C.: American University, June 19–21.

Rummel, R. S. 1976. "Understanding Factor Analysis." *The Journal of Conflict Resolution.* Vol. 11, No. 4.

Rural Development Act of 1972. 1973. Public Law 92–418, 86 STAT 657, Vols. 1 *and 2. U.S. Code: Congressional & Administrative News.* St. Paul, Minn., and Brooklyn, N.Y.: West Publishing Company and Charles Thompson Company.

Rural Policy Development Act of 1980. 1981. Public Law 96–355, 94 STAT 1171, Vol. 1. *U.S. Code: Congressional & Administrative News.* St. Paul, Minn.: West Publishing Company.

Rural Public Transportation in Pennsylvania. 1977. Harrisburg, Penn.: Pennsylvania Department of Transportation, Bureau of Advance Planning.

Rural Transportation in Pennsylvania: Problems and Prospects, Vol. 2. 1974. Report of the Governor's Task Force, Rural Transportation. Pennsylvania Department of Transportation.

Saltzman, Arthur. 1975. "Role of Paratransit in Rural Transportation." *Paratransit.* National Research Council, Transportation Research Board. Proceedings of a Conference sponsored by the Urban Mass Transportation Administration held November 9–12, Washington, D.C.

Saltzman, Arthur; Blair, Marion R.; Johnson, Joyce; Binstock, Deborah; and Burkhardt, Jon. 1974. "Rural Public Transportation Systems Feasibility Study: A Progress Report." Greensboro: Transportation Institute, North Carolina Agricultural and Technical State University.

Seegrist, Eileen. 1981. Chairman, Atlanta Heritage Trust. "Neighborhood Revitalization in Neartown, Atlanta." Presentation to the Georgia Chapter Planners Luncheon. Atlanta, February 19.

Shishkin, Julius. 1976. "Employment and Unemployment: The Donut or the Hole?" *Monthly Labor Review.* Washington, D.C.: U.S. Department of Labor, Bureau of Labor Statistics. February.

Sirageldin, Ishmail Abdel-Hamid. 1969. *Non-Market Components of National Income.* Ann Arbor: Institute for Social Research, Surrey Research Center, University of Michigan.

Skinner, B. F. 1953. *Science and Human Behavior.* London: Free Press.

Skorpa, Lidnard; Dodge, Richard; Walton, C. Michael; and Huddleston, John.

1974. "Transportation Impact Studies: A Review with Emphasis on Rural Areas." Austin: Council of Advanced Transportation Studies, University of Texas.

South Carolina Economic Trends. 1968. July.

Southern Regional Council. 1977. *Increasing the Options: A Report of the Task Force on Southern Rural Development.* Atlanta.

Stafford, Howard A. 1974. "The Anatomy of the Location Decision: Content Analysis of Case Studies." Cited in F. E. Hamilton, *Spatial Perspectives on Industrial Organization and Decision Making.* New York: John Wiley & Sons.

Stockman, David. 1981. Director, U.S. Office of Management and Budget. Interview with Robin MacNeil, "MacNeil/Lehrer Report," *PBS.* WETA Television, Athens/Atlanta, Ga., February 19.

Stopher, Peter. 1974. "Derivation of Values of Time from Travel Demand Models." *Transportation Research Record 587.* Washington, D.C.: National Research Council.

Stubbs, Anne. 1976. *State Community Development Policy: The Case of New Communities.* Lexington, Ky.: Council of State Governments.

Summers, Gene F., and Lang, Jean M. 1976. "Bringing Jobs to People: Does It Pay?" *Small Town.* Ellensberg, Wash.: Small Towns Institute.

Surface Transportation Act of 1978. 1979. Public Law 95-599, 92 STAT 2689, Vol. 2. *U.S. Code: Congressional & Administrative News.* St. Paul, Minn.: West Publishing Company.

"The Survey of Buying Power Data Service 1977." 1978. *Sales & Marketing Management.*

Svercl, Paul V., and Asin, Ruth H. 1973. "Home-to-Work Trips and Travel." *Nationwide Personal Transportation Study.* Report No. 8. U.S. Department of Transportation, Federal Highway Administration.

Sweet, David C., and Maggied, Hal S. 1967. "An Analysis of a Port's Hinterland." *Battelle Technical Review* (May).

Sweet, David C., et al. 1969. "The Potential for High Technology Industries in the Coastal Plains Region." Prepared by Battelle Memorial Institute, Columbus, Ohio, for the Coastal Plains Regional Commission, January 13.

Taafe, Edward J., and Gauthier, Howard L. 1973. *Geography of Transportation.* Englewood Cliffs, N.J.: Prentice-Hall.

Tartar, Barry. 1976. Director, Planning Division, North Georgia Area Planning and Development Commission. Personal interview, Cartersville, Ga., October 15.

Tarver, James D. 1973. "Patterns of Population Change among Southern Non-Metropolitan Towns, 1950-1970." *Rural Sociology* 37 (March).

Threlkeld, Richard. 1978. "Item on Family Income." *CBS Morning News.* New York, October 25.

Toner, Bill. 1977. "A New Word for 'Micropolitan' Planners." *Planning* 43 (July):37.

Tyner, Hugh. 1980. Chief, Research and Development Bureau, Georgia Department of Transportation. Personal conversation, Washington, D.C., January 24.

U.S. Congress. 1968. Senate. Subcommittee on Employment and Manpower of the

Committee on Labor and Public Welfare. *Toward Full Employment: Proposals for a Comprehensive Employment and Manpower Policy in the United States.*

———. 1974a. Senate. Subcommittee on Rural Development, Committee on Agriculture and Forestry. *The Effects of Uncertain Energy Supplies on Rural Economic Development.*

———. 1974b. Senate. Subcommittee on Rural Development, Committee on Agriculture and Forestry. *The Transportation of People in Rural Areas: Rural Transit Needs, Operations, and Management.*

———. 1975. Senate. National Area Development Institute, Congressional Research Service. *Prelude to Legislation to Solve the Growing Crisis in Rural Transportation, Part II — Meeting Rural Transportation Needs.* Prepared for the Committee on Agriculture and Forestry. February 10.

U.S. Department of Agriculture. 1972. Economic Development Division, Economic Research Service. *Characteristics of U.S. Rural Areas with Noncommuting Population.* Prepared for the Senate Committee on Agriculture and Forestry, Committee Print. Washington, D.C.: U.S. Government Printing Office.

———. 1974. "Social and Labor Adjustment of Rural Black Americans in the Mississippi Delta: A Case Study of Madison, Arkansas." December.

———. 1981. "Implementation of the Small Community and Rural Development Policy." Part I. Report from the Secretary to the President. Washington, D.C.

U.S. Department of Agriculture and U.S. Department of Transportation. 1980. "Agricultural Transportation Services: Needs, Problems, Opportunities." Final Report of the Rural Transportation Advisory Task Force, Washington, D.C.

U.S. Department of Commerce, Bureau of Census. 1969. *Current Population Reports.* Series P-20, No. 189. Cited in Eyestone (1972).

———. 1970a. "Census Users Dictionary." *1970 Census Users' Guide.* Part 1. Washington, D.C.: U.S. Government Printing Office.

———. 1970b. "Place of Work for Regions, Divisions & States: 1970." *General Social and Economic Characteristics.* PC(1)-Cl. U.S. Summary, Table 151. Washington, D.C.: U.S. Government Printing Office.

———. 1971a. "Final Population Counts: Advance Report." *1970 Census of Population.* PC(VI)-12, Georgia. Washington, D.C.: U.S. Government Printing Office.

———. 1971b. *Statistical Abstract of the United States: 1970.* Washington, D.C.: U.S. Government Printing Office.

———. 1973a. "Detailed Economic and Social Characteristics." *United States Census of Population: 1970.* Vol. 1, Part 12, Georgia.

———. 1973b. "General Population Characteristics." *United States Census of Population: 1970.* Vol. 1, Part 12, Georgia; Part 1. U.S.

———. 1973c. "Housing Characteristics for States, Cities, and Counties." *1970 Census of Population.* Vol. 1.

———. 1975. *Statistical Abstract of the United States: 1974.* Washington, D.C.: U.S. Government Printing Office.

———. 1977a. "Population Estimates and Projections." *Current Population Reports.* Series P-25, No. 658. Washington, D.C.: U.S. Government Printing Office.

———. 1977b. *Statistical Abstract of the United States: 1976.* Washington, D.C.: U.S. Government Printing Office.

———. 1978a. *County and City Data Book, 1977.* (A Statistical Abstract Supplement.) Washington, D.C.: U.S. Government Printing Office.

———. 1978b. "Place of Work Information." *The 1970 Census of Population and Housing.* Technical Department No. 8, Fifth Count Census Tape, Tabulation 35, Special Run, Georgia.

———. 1978c. "Selected Characteristics of Travel to Work in 21 Metropolitan Areas: 1975." *Current Population Reports.* Washington, D.C.: U.S. Government Printing Office.

———. 1978d. *Statistical Abstract of the United States: 1977.* Washington, D.C.: U.S. Government Printing Office.

———. 1981. *Statistical Abstract of the United States: 1980.* Washington, D.C.: U.S. Government Printing Office.

U.S. Department of Labor, Bureau of Labor Statistics. 1970. *Employment and Training Report of the President.* Washington, D.C.: U.S. Government Printing Office.

———. 1971. *Employment and Training Report of the President.* Washington, D.C.: U.S. Government Printing Office.

———. 1972. *Employment and Training Report of the President.* Washington, D.C.: U.S. Government Printing Office.

———. 1973. *Employment and Training Report of the President.* Washington, D.C.: U.S. Government Printing Office.

———. 1974. *Employment and Training Report of the President.* Washington, D.C.: U.S. Government Printing Office.

———. 1975. *Geographic Profile of Employment.* Washington, D.C.: U.S. Government Printing Office.

———. 1976. *Geographic Profile of Employment.* Washington, D.C.: U.S. Government Printing Office.

———. 1977. "Historical Report on Labor Force and Employment." Bureau in-house work tables, transmitted by Patricia Nielson, Atlanta.

U.S. Department of Transportation. 1972. *Conference on Transportation and Human Needs in the '70's.* Washington, D.C.: American University.

———. 1974. Federal Highway Administration. *Social and Economic Effects of Highways.* Washington, D.C.: Office of Program and Policy Planning, Socio-Economic Studies Division.

———. 1976a. *National Transportation Trends and Choices (to the Year 2000).* Washington, D.C.: U.S. Government Printing Office.

———. 1976b. *Proceedings of the First National Conference on Rural Public Transportation.* Greensboro, N.C.

————. 1976c. Office of Technology Sharing. *Rural Passenger Transportation —
Technology Sharing: State-of-the-Art Overview.* Technology Sharing Program
Office, Transportation Systems Center, Cambridge, Mass.

————. 1976d. Urban Mass Transportation Administration. *Urban Mass Transpor-
tation Act of 1964 and Related Laws.* Public Law 88–365, 78 STAT 302, 49
U.S.C. 1601 et seq. No. 05–014–00007–0. Washington, D.C.: U.S. Government
Printing Office.

————. 1976e. Urban Mass Transportation Administration. *Urban Mass Transportation Act of 1964 and Related Laws.* Section 16d as added by Section 8 of Public
Law 91–453 (as amended through February 5, 1976).

————. 1977a. Office of Secretary, Office of R&D Policy. *Rural Passenger Transportation Primer.* Cambridge, Mass.

————. 1977b. Office of the Secretary, Office of R&D Policy. *Toward 2000: Opportunities in Transportation Evolution.* Washington, D.C.: U.S. Government
Printing Office.

————. 1977c. Planning Data Services Section. "Mileage of Public Roads in Georgia
Classified by Highway District, County, Surface Type, and System." DPP
Statistical Report No. 441–D–77. Atlanta.

————. 1979. Office of Intergovernmental Affairs. *Through Their Eyes: Providing
Transportation for Rural Americans.* Part IV, No. 281–568/138. Washington,
D.C.: U.S. Government Printing Office.

U.S. General Accounting Office. 1977. *Hindrances to Coordinating Transportation
of People Participating in Federally Funded Grant Programs.* Vols. 1 and 2, CED
77–119. Washington, D.C.: U.S. Government Printing Office.

University of Georgia. 1976. College of Business Administration, Division of Research. *1976 Georgia Statistical Abstract.* Atlanta.

————. 1979. Geography Department, Electro-Data Processing Computer Printout, Factor Analysis. Athens, Ga., April 1–9.

Urban Mass Transportation Act of 1964. 1965. Public Law 88–365, 78 STAT 302,
Vol. 2. *U.S. Code: Congressional & Administrative News.* St. Paul, Minn., and
Brooklyn, N.Y.: West Publishing Company and Edward Thompson Company.

Urban Mass Transportation Act of 1966. 1967. Public Law 89–562, 80 STAT 715,
Vol. 2. *U.S. Code: Congressional & Administrative News.* St. Paul, Minn., and
Brooklyn, N.Y.: West Publishing Company and Charles Thompson Company.

Urban Mass Transportation Assistance Act of 1970. 1971. Public Law 91–453, 84
STAT 962, Vols. 1 and 2. *U.S. Code: Congressional & Administrative News.* St.
Paul, Minn., and Brooklyn, N.Y.: West Publishing Company and Charles
Thompson Company.

Von Neumann, John, and Morgenstern, Oskar. 1953. *The Theory of Games and
Economic Behavior.* Princeton, N.J.: Princeton University Press.

Wagner, Tom. 1978. Data Center Coordinator, Georgia Office of Planning and
Budget, State Data Center, Atlanta. Conference, October 10.

Wallace, Gene. 1978. Georgia Department of Education, Atlanta. Telephone conversation, October 14.

Wallace, Richard S., and Lemly, James H. 1969. "Analysis of Economic Impact of Highway Change on Two Small Georgia Communities." GHC Research Project HPS-1(50). Prepared for the State Highway Department of Georgia.

Ward, J. D.; O'Leary, K. L.; Chu, S. C.; Linhares, A. B.; Ryan, D. C., Jr.; and Maio, D. J. 1977. *Toward 2000: Opportunities in Transportation Evolution.* U.S. Department of Transportation, Office of the Secretary. Washington, D.C.: Office of R&D Research.

Watson, Donald Stevenson, ed. 1965. *Price Theory in Action, A Book of Readings.* Washington, D.C.: George Washington University Press.

Webber, Melvin. 1978. "Technics and Ethics in Transport Decision." *Transportation and Land Development Conference Proceedings.* Washington, D.C.: Transportation Research Board.

Wellslager, O. M. "Zckc." 1978. Coastal Plains Regional Commission, Charleston, S.C. Personal conference, November 28.

Wheeler, James O. 1974. *The Urban Circulation Noose.* No. Scituate, Mass.: Duxbury Press.

Whisman, John D. 1970a. States' regional representative, Appalachian Regional Commission. Project Meeting, Washington, D.C., May.

———. 1970b. Governor's alternate, Appalachian Regional Commission. Meeting, Washington, D.C., September.

Whittington, Susan. 1976–1979. Georgia Department of Human Resources, Office of Aging, Atlanta. Intermittent telephone conversations, November 1976–April 1979.

Whittington, Susan, and Whittington, Frank. 1975. *Georgia's Older Population — A Data Book on Aging.* Atlanta: Georgia Department of Human Resources, Office of Aging.

Wildavsky, Aaron. 1974. *The Politics of the Budgetary Process,* 2nd ed. Boston: Little, Brown.

Work in America. 1973. Report of a Special Task Force to the Secretary of Health, Education, and Welfare. Prepared under the auspices of W. E. Upjohn Institute of Employment Research. Cambridge, Mass.: MIT Press.

INDEX

AUTHOR INDEX

SUBJECT INDEX